TO BELIEVE OR NOT BELIEVE, THAT IS THE QUESTION:

AN UNDERCOVER AGENT'S QUEST FOR THE TRUTH

—⁓—

BY
THOMAS J. GORMAN

PRESS

TO BELIEVE OR NOT BELIEVE,
THAT IS THE QUESTION:
AN UNDERCOVER AGENT'S QUEST
FOR THE TRUTH
by Thomas J. Gorman

Printed in the United States of America

ISBN 978-1-60034-988-1

Unless otherwise indicated, Bible quotations are taken from New American Standard Bible. Copyright © 1977 by Thomas Nelson Publishers Nashville, Camden and New York. If a different version is used, the abbreviations for that version will follow the citation for the book, chapter and verse(s). New International Version will be abbreviated (NI) and the New Living Translation (NL)

www.xulonpress.com

CONTENTS

—ɯ—

DEDICATION

—⁓—

This book is dedicated to our grandchildren; Matt, Jake, Blake and Alyssa. Our prayers are that you always walk with the Lord, and devote your lives to making this a better world.

ACKNOWLEDGMENTS

—⁓—

I would like to thank my sisters, Pat Burton and Irene Lalich for helping to edit my draft manuscript. A thank you to Barry Jamison for being candid about my first attempt at writing this book. He suggested that I personalize the story which lead to Part One. Barry also helped edit. A special thanks to all those in the "Early Risers" Adult Bible Fellowship who encouraged me to put my class notes into book form. I especially want to thank my wife for being instrumental in changing my life, and for all her sacrifices. I was truly, *Touched by an Angel.* Lastly, I thank God for all the undeserved blessings and the gift of salvation.

This book only touches the surface of many important topics. It is simply an executive summary or synopsis of the hard work and research of others. Hopefully, the book will motivate you to increase your knowledge of Christian apologetics. I strongly encourage you to review the list of reference material and read some if not all of the books listed. Your confidence in discussing Christianity will increase substantially.

I would like to acknowledge and thank the authors of the reference material that I used to write this book. They are the ones that did the research, so this topic could be presented factually. They are the ones that have touched so many lives. They are the ones that helped me understand and accept Christianity. These authors have used their God given gifts to further the kingdom. What a great ministry! A special thanks to Josh McDowell for his in-depth research, hard work, and great books.

PART ONE

THE INVESTIGATION

CHAPTER 1

INTRODUCTION

—ᴍᴌ—

I usually don't read all the material at the beginning of a book. I generally find the acknowledgements, preface, and dedication boring, so I usually go right to the first chapter. Since I like to think of myself as an average, normal kind of person (regardless of what my wife might say), I figure a lot of you do the same thing. Well surprise! This is actually the preface disguised as the first chapter. Stop! Don't turn to chapter two. I would appreciate your reading this section. I think it's important to help understand and follow this book.

To Believe or Not Believe, That is the Question: An Undercover Agent's Quest for the Truth is divided into three parts. Part one is the story of how I, an agnostic law enforcement officer, investigated Christianity to see if sufficient evidence existed to convict that religion of being what it claimed to be. Part two contains most of the detailed evidence I found during my two-year investigation. Part three attempts to provide some answers to difficult questions often asked about Christianity.

I hope this book will compel doubters to conduct their own investigation, or objectively consider the evidence presented and its application to their lives. I also hope this book will increase the knowledge and confidence level of Christians, to better explain and share their faith with skeptics.

Your spiritual life and relationship to God is an important aspect of both living and dying. If you haven't already, you might want to consider basing your beliefs on sound evidence and logic, rather than simply on something that "feels right." Many people have created self-made religions, buffet style, which includes a little bit of this and a little bit of that. My experience has been that they cannot support what they believe with solid evidence and logic.

Try to read this book objectively and examine the evidence carefully. You don't have to agree with everything. Some points may not be very convincing to you. That's fine. However, try not to let that distract you from considering the preponderance of evidence presented, or other parts of an answer to a question. Like a juror during a trial, you don't have to accept all the evidence. But, you do have to decide, if overall there is sufficient direct and/or circumstantial evidence to reach a conclusion beyond a reasonable doubt.

In order to set a foundation to begin this book, I should mention that I began drifting away from Christianity and a belief in a personal God at the "mature age" of thirteen. Subsequent university classes seemed to destroy any possible chance I would have to believe the Bible, upon which much of Christianity is based. After twelve years as a special agent with the California Department of Justice, I began my most significant and important investigation. Through a rather strange series of events, I decided to examine the evidence, if any existed, to determine if there was any validity to what those Christians believed.

CHAPTER 2

IN THE BEGINNING

—⁓—

Since this is my first attempt at writing non-law enforcement material, I asked some friends for suggestions. My initial question was, "How do I begin the first chapter about my life?" One creative type who is a little left-of-center suggested that I start at the end and work backwards. That was an interesting concept, but seemed strange. I thought that perhaps the end should come at the end. Remember I'm a cop; we don't tend to think like artistic types. Besides, I'm still alive so the end isn't even here yet! Another suggestion was to start where I begin to formulate the theme of the book. I took that to mean that I should start where I begin making my point to the reader. The problem with that technique was that most readers would probably want to know how I got to that point in the first place. Confused? Me too! Most suggested that I simply start at or near the beginning. That made sense to me so I decided to follow their advice.

The Old Testament starts by saying, "In the beginning God created the heavens and earth …" I should point out that some believe; in the beginning a *Big Bang* started the universe and life. I guess using either one of those as a starting point for this book is probably going back too far.

How's this? Thomas Joseph Gorman III was born in Atlantic City, New Jersey in June, 1943. I've been told that I'm a Gemini for those of you who follow astrology. Here's a little side note; Gemini is the twin and the name Thomas means twin. So, if you observe a little schizophrenia in my writing you'll understand that it's not my fault. I'm a victim of my name and those darn stars. Continuing, I led somewhat of a normal childhood considering that I had four brothers, two sisters, and a father who was a career military officer. During my first thirteen years, the family lived in eight different places, including two tours in Germany.

My Grandpop Gasko's South Jersey farm in Bear's Head, just outside of Mays Landing, was always home base. I was a gifted little left-handed athlete who played football, basketball, and baseball. I also boxed and ran track. I participated in both the Cub Scouts and Boy Scouts, even though I still can't tie a knot worth a darn, or make a fire by rubbing two sticks together. I played drums in the school band for a while, until the leader discovered that I was playing to the beat of a different drummer. The family attended Catholic Church where I was an altar boy. That was in the days when serving Mass meant learning Latin, ringing the bells at the exact right time, carrying that heavy Book with a bunch of Epistles and Gospels (whatever they were), and appearing pious. I was basically a good clean-cut All-American kid who had a great life. Either Bill Cosby or Ward Cleaver would have been proud to have had me as a son.

I loved the summers being a country boy in Bear's Head, but I also loved life living on a military base. There's nothing like watching soldiers marching and shouting cadence. At the end of the day, everyone on base stopped to honor the flag while "taps" was being played. Those military convoys with jeeps and big trucks were impressive. I looked forward to the Saturday matinee at the base theater watching news briefs, cartoons, a superman serial, and my favorite cowboy, Roy Rogers. I remember nights laying on the floor listening to *The Whistler* on the big console radio. I tuned in to New York Yankee baseball games whenever I could, hoping Mickey Mantle would belt another homer to beat the Red Sox. Sorry Boston fans, but the Bronx is closer to New Jersey than Massachusetts. I did like Ted Williams though.

Are you getting impatient? Are you wondering what Roy Rogers and Mickey Mantle have to do with Christianity? Fear not. I will get to my investigation of Christianity, but this background will help tie it all together. If you are really bored with all this background information, then go ahead and skip to Chapter 8.

Living in Germany was a great experience for a young boy. I loved the country and the German people. In kindergarten I met my first girlfriend,

Cookie Cobb. She was gorgeous. She was a blond just like my wife. I also have fond memories of my best German friend, "Boomsell Belly" (Big Belly). I think he ate too much of that good German food. At the age of four, we had our own language that no one else understood. It was called "Germerican." He was my "bestest" buddy who loved wearing his lederhosen and Barvarian hat. What a great life!

Back in New Jersey, I remember seeing television for the first time in Grandpop's front room while he smoked his pipe. I loved that smell. I also loved eating potato chips out of a big tin can, drinking 7-Up, and watching *Howdy Dowdy* on a nineteen-inch black and white console set. Life couldn't have been any better. Well, maybe swimming in the South River and catching tadpoles rivaled TV. Or, maybe it was kissing one of the Mattle girls. Was it Jeannie or Patti? Maybe both. Oh yeah, Bonnie Bergman was the love of my life too. I was quite a little Don Juan. I wasn't exactly tall, dark, and handsome, but I had my own style. Striped T-shirt, baggie blue jeans rolled up a couple inches, a belt two sizes too big, ball cap, and high-top black "Keds" sneakers. Sounds like a potential model for GQ magazine. Yes, I was quite a catch for those cute little country girls.

My family left New Jersey and moved to Fort Gordon, Georgia for my first experience living in the South. All nine of us lived in the second story of a military barracks building converted for families. This was the classic story of a young Yankee boy living in what many considered the Confederate States of America. I learned quickly that what I had always thought was the Civil War, was actually the War of Northern Aggression. I attended Blythe Elementary School and learned a new language. Just think, I was only in seventh grade and I could speak English, "Germerican," and "Georgian."

I loved my time in Georgia, especially once I agreed to burn my New Jersey birth certificate while singing *Dixie*. I certainly learned history from a different perspective. Did you know that General Sherman was a pyromaniac, or that General Lee actually won the Battle of Gettysburg? It was at Blythe School where I received the nickname, "Lefty." That was a sure sign of acceptance since everyone had either a nickname or two first names. I liked "Lefty" better than "Tommy Joe." I was there less than a year, but Principal Bowen and my classmates made me feel right at home. I even learned to like hushpuppies, black-eyed peas, grits, and boiled peanuts. I starred in flag football and basketball, and broke Richmond County's seventh grade record for the hundred-yard dash. I continued to wow the girls. I especially liked Edna Pittman, Bonnie Schofield, and the girl that was held back two years. I attended Catholic Mass at the post chapel and remained a good boy, except for a few impure thoughts about that well endowed fifteen-year old classmate. I imagine during confession Father Michael heard that from many of the young Catholic boys. Life was good! I was a happy, well-adjusted, all-American kid. Then suddenly my life took a drastic turn and everything changed almost overnight.

CHAPTER 3

LIFE CHANGING MOVE

—⟋⟍⟍⟋—

In the summer of 1956 we left the "Peach State," the home of baseball great Ty Cobb and rock n' roll icon Little Richard. We moved to the Southwest. What a culture shock! Lots of dirt, flash floods, and tumbleweeds. Why on earth would a cowboy want to sing about those weeds mixed with sand and dust blowing across the desert? To make things worse, we arrived in the middle of the 250th anniversary of Albuquerque. Talk about the Wild West! Billy the Kid and Poncho Villa were alive and well in New Mexico. I wondered what Old Mexico was like if this was the new part. I wasn't sure my all-American boy image would fit. Especially considering my butch haircut and J.C. Penny's bike with playing cards hitting the spokes. I soon learned I was right.

My first day at Monroe Junior High was a terrible experience. I was immediately pegged as a "square." Maybe my Roy Rogers lunch box was a bit much. I think I was the only kid riding a bike, particularly one with cards in the spokes. This was my first experience in a city school. I knew I hated it. Nobody welcomed me and a number of the students made fun of me. I felt humiliated and all alone. Maybe I would be accepted when I played football or made the honor roll. I wondered how long that would take. Unfortunately, time wasn't on my side.

On the second day, I walked to school and ditched my lunch box. My first class was in some portable buildings away from the main school building. I arrived a little early and the teacher, Mr. Prudent, must have been in the teacher's hideout or lounge as they called it. There was a group of *West Side Story* looking guys with "DA" (Duck's Tail) haircuts and black leather jackets standing around smoking cigarettes, and doing nasty things with the girls. All of a sudden one of the "cool cats" starting picking on a small kid, almost as square as I was. He pushed him to the ground, knocking off the frightened boy's glasses. That didn't seem right! I was taught to defend the defenseless. Wasn't that part of the Military Code of Honor?

Without much thought I yelled out, "Hey, leave him alone!" Oops! The bully turned toward me sneering, "Well if it isn't little Roy Rogers coming to the rescue." Everyone laughed and hooted. He started for me with his fists clenched and cocked, declaring his intention to beat me to a bloody pulp. I was scared and shaking, but knew neither Roy Rogers nor Mickey Mantle would approve of my running away. Maybe I would get lucky and the teacher would show up. Wrong! There he was, "Mr. Cool," right in front of me rearing back to land a blow to my somewhat freckled face.

He let loose with a roundhouse punch, which I immediately blocked with my left and countered with a couple of right jabs to his head. I then threw a left hook catching him on the nose, which resulted in blood streaming down his face. A couple more right jabs and then a left uppercut sent him to the ground with blood pouring from his nose and mouth. He didn't get back up. He just laid there in a daze; down for the count. My boxing experience served me well. I looked over at his buddies expecting an attack, but instead heard, "Wow, he cold-cocked Spider. Coolsville!" "The kid is tough." "He put him down."

The next thing I heard was, "Hey, daddy-o, how about a smoke?" I guess that meant I was accepted. Awkwardly I smoked my first Lucky Strike cigarette. My new friends thought I was "Coolsville." Anytime you were described with a "ville" on the end of the word that was generally good. Life was looking up. Actually, at age thirteen on that September day in "The Land of Enchantment" my life began taking the wrong turn.

With my father gone to Korea or somewhere, it was easy to take advantage of my very naïve mother. I let my hair grow long in a perfect DA with a little curl over my forehead. I used lots of Vaseline for that "cool" greasy look. I purchased a leather jacket, and picked up a switchblade from a guy in Martinez Town. I even made a "zip gun" (homemade gun) that didn't work, but looked good. I didn't pursue sports, but rather hung around with my new pals. We spent time stealing, vandalizing, and fighting. Suddenly, I was the punk bully picking on other kids. I had become a complete juvenile delinquent.

Being bad was hard at first since my Catholic upbringing had created a conscience. I remember not being able to sleep at night because I was immersed in guilty feelings. I'd lie in my bed staring at the ceiling with nagging thoughts of being infected with *mortal sin* (that's a felony not misdemeanor offense). The words to that simple nighttime prayer would have to change to, "Now I lay me down to sleep, I know that Satan my soul he'll keep. If I should die before I wake, a trip to hell I'm sure to make." Finally, after a couple weeks of this torture, I developed a solution. I used my defense mechanisms to block out the guilt, and to deny that a personal God existed. I reasoned that religion was just a bunch of rules created by men to regulate behavior.

That was the beginning of my twenty-five year journey as an agnostic. That was also the beginning of my separation from God and denial of Christianity. If there was a God, he really didn't care about this world or its people. If Jesus existed, he was simply a radical Jewish Rabbi. Maybe he was a holy man and religious leader but nothing more. The so-called "Holy Bible" was the Jewish and Christian equivalent of Greek mythology. Who needed any of that except for the young and the weak? Religion was a good crutch, but I didn't need one. I could take care of myself. I could have easily adopted the Frank Sinatra song, *I Did It My Way* if it had been written at that time. I had to settle for the less philosophical Elvis song from the movie, *King Creole* called, *Trouble*. It goes, "If you're looking for trouble you've come to the right place ..."

Okay readers, where do we go from here? We could proceed with my autobiography, but that's not the purpose of this book. We could skip to my investigation of Christianity, but you are probably curious how I went from a juvenile criminal to law enforcement officer. What started me back on the straight and narrow? Let's compromise and briefly cover the period of my life from age thirteen to thirty-eight.

CHAPTER 4

TEEN ANGEL

—〰—

I continued my bad-boy lifestyle progressing to auto theft and even contempt of court. Out of the blue, my interfering older sister, Pat, came home from Immaculata College and had me enrolled at St. Mary's High School in downtown Albuquerque. The school was over twelve miles from our Hoffmantown hangout called the "Creamery." I was incensed, and determined to get kicked out of this religious school, which had witches called nuns running the joint. These Sisters of Charity [HA!] weren't the least bit intimidated by me. However, I found them to be much more intimidating than the police. Witnessing these aliens monitoring the hallway wearing black costumes and dragging rosary beads was a scary sight, even for a tough guy. I wasn't allowed to wear my gang garb, which made it much harder to play a rebel. I settled in and at least during school hours behaved decently, except for monthly fights in the boy's restroom or the alley. I began playing football, resumed boxing, and also worked at a service station.

In my spare time I continued to hang with the gang. Then all of a sudden I had no more spare time.

I met and fell for a beautiful blonde (Teen Angel). That's right! A good Catholic girl named Denny. All my limited spare time was spent with my steady, who wore my ring around her neck. This was the beginning of my junior year, and I left all my juvenile delinquent "friends" except for my buddy Paul. My sister Pat, Sister Thomas Marion, Coach Babe Parenti, and Denny all influenced a substantial positive change in my life.

After I graduated from high school at seventeen, I returned to South Jersey. My Uncle Phil Tartaglione introduced me to a boxing trainer named Nick, who worked in a gym on the south side of Atlantic City. I wanted to be a featherweight contender by the time I was nineteen. However, when you are lying on your back and the guy above you is counting to ten, that's a bad sign. After a couple months of professional boxing, I decided that a career change was in order. Besides, Denny had promised to leave New Mexico and come to New Jersey as soon as she turned eighteen. I didn't think she would like seeing me bruised and bleeding every other week. We did reunite on September 5th, 1961, just three days after she turned eighteen. On her birthday, she boarded a Greyhound bus for a ride across country. We stayed in New Jersey at a relative's home for about a month. For some reason and I think it was age restrictions, we couldn't get married without parental consent. So we left and headed to Mexico where, on October 15th, we were married in Juarez, across the boarder from El

Paso, Texas. We didn't tell anyone we were married, nor did we live together. She returned home and went to work at a credit union. I moved into a duplex with a high school teacher named Bob. I began working two jobs so we could get our own place.

Six months later, after a Mel Torme concert on a Sunday in April, 1962, we were in a romantic mood. No one was home at the duplex and guess what? That's right! Denny (now called Denise) got pregnant. Thanks Mel, for the mood music! Our daughter, Terri is a precious jewel. We subsequently announced our marriage and moved into a tiny house behind another home. After working a variety of jobs from waiter to delivery boy, I decided it was time to think about a career. Vietnam was beginning to attract attention. I thought about being drafted into the Army and assigned to the infantry. Why fight in a muddy foxhole, eat K- Rations (now called MRE's), and march through enemy territory carrying sixty pounds on your back. I decided that I'd rather sleep at night after a good dinner, then get up and shoot at the enemy from a fast jet while thousands of feet in the air. I enrolled in Air Force ROTC at the University of New Mexico (UNM). Unfortunately, within a few months, I was told to leave for, "… not having an attitude in keeping with the standards of the United States Air Force." I know what you Army, Navy, and Marine types are thinking. You're right, I was pretty bad. I didn't realize the eagle insignia on the Colonel's shoulder didn't belong where I suggested he stick it. When I told Denise what had happened, my darling nineteen-year-old wife explained that I did have a "unique" attitude. She commented that maybe I should forget the military.

Denise suggested that with my background and "unique" attitude I should consider becoming an undercover police officer. I wasn't sure what that was. She explained it was a job where you get paid to pretend that you're a bad guy. You've got to be kidding! There's a job like that? An adult game of cops and robbers. What a great idea! However, I found out I would have to get my juvenile record expunged to qualify for police work.

I continued at UNM and at the age of twenty-one successfully petitioned the courts to have my juvenile record sealed. Poof, just like that I became a record-free all-American boy again. Life was great! I then enrolled at San Jose State University, California (SJS) in the Police Science program. Denise did the research on colleges just like she did on potential careers. What a great partner!

I graduated from SJS with a BS [how appropriate] degree. Within three months, I was hired as an undercover agent with the California Bureau of Narcotics Enforcement. We moved to Sacramento, California and had a son also named Thomas J. We knew instinctively that he would be special. We were living the American dream.

CHAPTER 5

SECRET AGENT MAN

—⁓—

Life as a state undercover agent during the late sixties and seventies was exciting. We could and did work all over California, from Siskiyou County in the northern region to the San Francisco Bay Area down to Southern California. I was fortunate enough to have worked in 53 of California's 58 counties. My roles and situations varied. At times I would play an "acid" (LSD) using burned-out hippie trying to "score" from the so-called flower children in San Francisco's Haight-Ashbury area. Most of the time I played the role of an outlaw biker type. I had long hair and a grubby beard. Picture a seedy and slovenly looking character with an open cut-off denim jacket, no shirt underneath, and chains hanging around the neck. Yes, that was me. My nickname was "Pig Pen." There were times when Denise asked me to change clothes in the garage before I came into the house.

My previous life experiences helped me succeed as an undercover cop. Sometimes I would buy drugs or weapons, and at other times I would pose as a "hit" man. In all, I was able to make over 1,000 undercover purchases of contraband during a thirteen year period. Undercover work is very much like acting, although you don't get retakes. It's got to be right the first time. Also, the supporting cast is critical to a successful operation. A special thanks to all of you who covered my back and protected me. Thanks for being willing to put your life on the line to protect mine.

I didn't work undercover continuously for the entire thirteen years. I spent eighteen months at the Department of Justice Advanced Training Center teaching undercover techniques, officer survival, and drug identification. Eventually, I was promoted to supervisor, but continued to do some undercover work. This was especially true if I felt the crook was particularly dangerous, or the case needed a more experienced undercover agent. I loved my work, my family, and my life.

Oh yeah, I almost forgot, besides having a $25,000 contract placed on my life, I was awarded two purple hearts from the State of California. I was shot once in the chest, and then later stabbed in the right thigh. How Denise put up with all that I'll never know. She was, and continues to be, a true partner. I felt at the time that being wounded kind of made up for not serving in Vietnam with the thousands of true American heroes. Not serving is one of my life's regrets. I have the utmost respect for our veterans, especially those that served during wars and conflicts. I thank all of you for your unselfish sacrifice and courage.

This secret agent man continued as a closet agnostic, but agreed with Denise that our children should go to church. Our motives were somewhat different. Denise wanted Terri and Tom to be raised as Roman Catholics. I didn't care what faith, religion, or church they attended, just as long as they didn't become delinquents. Being a cop, I knew that kids who went to church generally got into less trouble, experienced less premarital sex and were less likely to use drugs. I regarded religion as an instrument of environment control, helping to get our children through their youth with minimal problems. It was similar to sending them to the best schools. I figured once they were eighteen they could believe whatever they wanted. I really didn't care what they chose. My motive was simply the advantages church life afforded young people.

Denise continued to go to church and was somewhat of a religious person. We had a very close and loving relationship in spite of our religious differences. To top it off, we were best friends. Much of the credit goes to Denise. OK, almost all of the credit goes to her. She gave much more than I deserved. Just ask our friends and my co-workers. Denise was, and is, a great mom. Just ask Terri and Tom.

CHAPTER 6

BORN-AGAIN WIFE

—⁓—

In 1978, Denise was working part time as a teacher's aide at Cordova Lane Elementary School, Rancho Cordova, California. Two of the teachers with whom she worked were very devout evangelical Christians. In the mornings, before class would start, Ray Peterson and Barbara Shinn discussed the Bible and Jesus. Denise listened to their discussions and eventually began asking questions. She wanted to know more about a personal relationship with Christ. After a couple of months, she made a conscious decision to confirm that she had given her life to Jesus. She had a born-again Christian experience.

That night she announced to me that she had become a born-again Christian. I know she wanted me to be happy for her, but I was upset. How could she do that to me? My immediate reaction was, there goes our sex life. I wasn't sure how or how often Christians engaged in sex, but I was sure it was infrequent and unexciting. How could she threaten our marriage like that without even asking how I felt?

Yeah, it was all about me! I just knew that our life was going to change and for the worst. She'd probably be praying and reading the Bible all the time. She would probably nag me about the language I used when our kids were not around, as well as my drinking and smoking. She would probably start citing Bible verses, and going around the house singing *Amazing Grace*, which I felt should be reserved for bag pipes at police funerals.

How to counter this dramatic change in my wife and set her straight became my new mission. I began attacking Christianity and her faith with very negative and sarcastic comments like, "Denise how can you believe all that stuff? You're too smart to be sucked in. Religion is fine for the weak and needy, but you're not one of them. Why do you insist in reading that Bible? You've got to know it's full of myths and errors. If your God is so loving, why do good people suffer? How can a loving God send people to hell? The idea of heaven and an involved god or gods was invented by rulers to keep people in line." I was relentless in my attacks, but Denise remained sweet and loving. She seemed to be at peace. She would tell me that she didn't know all the answers, but knew in her heart that her faith was real. She knew Jesus was her Lord and Savior. She was hooked and no amount of haranguing or, what I considered rational thinking, was going to change her. Thank God, she was still enjoyable to be with. At least she didn't change in that regard. I finally decided to let it go. If it made her happy and didn't interfere with our relationship, why should I care?

At least I wouldn't be taken in by all that Christian nonsense. Little did I know that sweet little Denise had planned a counter-attack.

CHAPTER 7

COUNTER-ATTACK

—ᜠ—

Between a very demanding job with long hours, and my desire to be an engaged husband and father I led a very hectic life. The bathroom became my favorite refuge. It was a good place to relax. Often, I would read one of the magazines left near the commode. I wasn't particular. Either the R*eader's Digest* or *Sports Illustrated* would be fine. I just wanted a few uninterrupted minutes to myself. One evening after dinner, I retreated to my little hide-away and sat down, only to discover there were no magazines to be found. The only thing to read was a pamphlet about the Bible's Book of Revelations. Oh well, at least it was something to read. Being very curious and a history buff, it was actually an interesting fictional account of what Christians believed were the signs of the end of the world. It covered things like the Anti-Christ, the sign of the beast (666), and the Battle of Armageddon. Fascinating stuff! It was kind of a Biblical version of *Star Wars*. I spent about ten minutes reviewing the pamphlet.

When I left the bathroom, I asked Denise, "Hey Babe, what happened to the magazines you usually leave in our bathroom?" She matter-of-factly responded, "I took them out and must have forgotten to put them back. Sorry!" She didn't mention the Bible material nor did I. This "bait and switch" scam continued with different Christian material on the "end of time." One evening while I was reading about the rapture, a fleeting thought crossed my mind, "There are actually some intelligent and sophisticated people that call themselves Christians. What if what Christians believe is true? I'll be in deep trouble."

Finally, after the third time of missing my normal reading material, I caught on to Denise's plot. After all, I'm a trained special agent. Enough is enough! I went to Denise and told her that I was wise to her game and it wouldn't work. I asked her to put the *Reader's Digest* and *Sports illustrated* back, and to stop promoting that Christian propaganda. I wasn't buying all that end of the world junk and never would.

Denise not-so-calmly countered with, "You know, for someone who prides himself in being so objective, you are actually extremely close-minded. When it comes to Christianity, somehow you think you know it all. You haven't even read the Bible, which you are so fond of criticizing. You must have a special gift that doesn't require critical thinking. Just think it and it's right. I sure hope you handle your investigations with a little more objectivity. In fact, since you are such a hot shot special agent, why don't you investigate Christianity? You could either prove or disprove it once and for all. Or are you afraid of what you will find? It's probably easier just to indict without bothering to consider any evidence. I'm getting tired of your self-righteous negativism!"

Wow! Where did that come from? Was that Denise challenging me? She was serious! Maybe I pushed her too far and she's pushing back. I wasn't going to let her win this one so I responded, "You're on! If you promise that when I'm finished investigating your faith, you will be open to listening to the results. If I can disprove Christianity, you must agree that you won't ever mention it to me again." Surprisingly, she quickly agreed. I then began an investigation of my most important case. I was going, to once and for all, show the fallacy of the Christian faith.

CHAPTER 8

OPENING A CASE

—∿∿—

Almost immediately, I was sorry I let Denise talk me into this project. It would be very time consuming. I already knew the outcome, namely that there is no real evidence to support Christianity. It wasn't as if I had a lot of time to prove something I already believed. However, I did make a deal with my wife.

The question was, where do I begin to disprove Christianity? Suddenly a random thought crossed my mind that shed light on my approach. A good investigator doesn't have his or her mind made up before initiating an investigation. Good investigators are supposed to remain neutral and objective throughout the case. We are trained to let the evidence and facts lead to probable cause and the suspect. It's not supposed to be the other way around. Yet, as Denise had pointed out, I had convicted Christianity before my investigation even began. If I conducted my research as I was trained, I would look into this case objectively without a preconceived conclusion.

I would let the facts and evidence acquit or convict Christianity of being a fraud.

Once I made up my mind to pursue this research like a real investigation, I needed a starting point. My Catholic background gave me a fairly good grasp of what Christians believed. I could still recite most of the "Apostles Creed" with words like, "I believe in God the Father almighty ... and in Jesus Christ, His only Son ... was crucified, died and was buried ... He rose again from the dead ... I believe in the ... forgiveness of sin, the resurrection of the body, and life everlasting."

How, when, where, and why did Christians formulate those beliefs? I would have to go back to the beginning of their religion. What did they use as their primary source or sources? The answer was clear. It was the teachings of Jesus and the Bible, particularly the New Testament. I remembered that Jesus, with the help of the apostles, actually started the religion that spread across the world.

Most of what is known about Jesus and the early Church can be found in the Bible. So, my first task would be to learn more about the Bible. Who wrote it? Who put it together? Who decided it was holy? Is it really unique and one-of-a-kind? After I gathered the basic facts, I would then examine the Bible itself to determine whether it is reliable, accurate, and trustworthy, or full of errors, inaccuracies, and distortions. I would need to answer the question; is the Bible a reliable historic document or a book of myths? Thus my primary focus would be on the founder of the religion, Jesus, and the primary historical documentation on which the religion is based, the Bible. My investigation would consist of reading volumes of material on the Bible and Jesus, as well as interviewing subject matter experts.

For this part of the book and ease of reading, I will present most of my investigation in an interview format. Some of these discussions actually took place, while others did not. However, all that follows does reflect what I found in my research. Part Two of this book has the more detailed research material and appropriate references.

My preliminary inquiry led to some interesting facts about the Bible. I refer to them as facts because there doesn't appear to be any opposition to their claim of accuracy. These facts include:

- The Bible was written over a time span of about 1,500 years.
- There were approximately 40 different authors who wrote parts of the Bible.
- The Bible is divided into two major parts; the Old and New Testaments.
- Both the Old and New Testaments are further divided into smaller books. The New has 27 books and the Old has 39 books.
- The Old Testament was written in Hebrew (Jewish language) and the New Testament was written in the universal language of the day, Greek.
- The Jewish Old Testament is the same document that Christians use except the books are counted differently.
- The Bible is the best selling book of all time.

- The central theme of the Bible is God's relationship to mankind.

During the preliminary phase of my inquiry, I wondered how the different books written over so many years and by so many authors ended up in the Bible. My conversation with a theologian on this issue is summarized below.

After some get-acquainted small talk, I asked, "Can you explain to me who was responsible for, and what process was used to determine which books would be included in the Bible?"

Without hesitation he answered, "The canons of the Old and New Testament were established by different persons at different times using slightly different criteria. The __"

I interrupted, "Excuse me, but would you please explain what you mean by canon?"

Apologetically he responded, "I'm sorry. I shouldn't have assumed you knew the definition of canon. We theologians tend to have our own terminology much like you in the police profession. Canon denotes the officially accepted books of Holy Scripture. It comes from the root word, *reed.* The reed was used as a standard measuring rod. Thus canon is the standard."

"Thanks. I'll probably be asking lots of questions as we go along. Let's get back to how it was decided which books to accept as part of the Bible."

"Jewish religious leaders conducted extensive research, and carefully examined the manuscripts included in their religious scrolls. They didn't actually possess books during that period. They used scrolls which were strips of glue sheets of their paper wound around a rod. In order to read the scroll, a priest would have to unroll them to the place where the reading would begin. Now, getting back to how they determined which manuscripts to accept. The leaders only accepted those documents they considered written by people of God that were consistent with Jewish religious teachings, and were inspired by God."

"That's a very general and subjective criteria. Is there any support for those manuscripts other than the Jewish leaders?"

He paused a moment. "Yes. In fact, Jesus himself accepted the Old Testament as Holy Scripture, as did the apostles and early church leaders."

I challenged his using Jesus as a witness. "No offense meant by this, but it hardly seems that a Jewish Rabbi and his band of followers would be considered objective witnesses to the document that established their religion. They would have no personal knowledge, but rather be relying on what was passed down through the generations. All Jewish boys from the time they could learn were told the Old Testament was Scripture. In fact, it was part of their ceremony into manhood. Jesus and his followers would not be credible witnesses. A court of law would not accept their hearsay testimony on behalf of the Old Testament."

Shaking his head he fired back, "Are you telling me that the Son of God is an unreliable witness?"

"I would first have to believe that Jesus was the Son of God which, in my mind, hasn't been established. That's down the road in my investigation. Do you have anything else?"

He immediately answered, "As a matter of fact I do. If you examine the books that comprise the Old Testament, I believe you would have to conclude they are unique, one-of-a-kind, and could only exist with the aid of God. How else do you explain the accuracy of prophecies in material written thousands of years ago?"

Trying to stay with the current subject I responded, "I plan on carefully examining the contents of the Bible but haven't done so yet. I'll have to reserve judgement until that time. Let's get back to the cannon of the Bible. How were the New Testament books determined?"

He graciously continued, "We have more information about the New Testament for obvious reasons. After Christ's death, a number of letters and gospels were written. Between A.D. 90 and 397, church leaders studied, examined, and tested those writings for inclusion in the Bible. The process began at the Council of Jamnia and finally concluded at the Council of Carthage. Most of the books were selected by A.D. 200. There were a few that were disputed. Some of the tests used included: 1) Written by an apostle or under the authority of an apostle. 2) Must accurately reflect the teachings and life of Jesus. 3) Written when witnesses to the events were still living. 4) Accepted by the followers of Jesus. 5) Historically and geographically accurate. 6) Inspired by God."

"You're right. You do have more detail regarding the New Testament books. However, like the Old

Testament, it is still very subjective. I admit based on what you have told me, there is more support for the New than the Old Testament. The fact that witnesses to the recorded events were still living tends to lend credibility to the tests used by the early church. That is, unless I find historic documents from that time saying what was written was false. I heard there were other gospels discovered that weren't included in the Bible. Wasn't there Gospels of both Thomas and Peter that were rejected?"

He leaned forward in his chair. "You're referring to the Gnostic Gospels. They were written in the second century by a semi-religious movement related to Christianity. This movement called Gnosticism taught salvation could only be achieved by acquiring knowledge. They taught a revised theology with a rather remote god. To support their new theology, they wrote books which were found in 1945 in Egypt. These books were written 100 to 200 years after the death of Jesus. None were authored by the persons for whom they were named, since they were all dead when the books were written. The books were very mystic in nature with many false teachings and errors."

At that time I had no other questions. I stood up and shook his hand. "This has been interesting! Dan (my friend who arranged the meeting with this theologian) was right. You are very knowledgeable. Thanks for your help and the information. If it's okay, I would like to contact you again after I do more research."

He shook my hand and smiled. "My pleasure. You are welcome to contact me anytime. Please don't hesitate to call. I look forward to the next time."

CHAPTER 9

INVESTIGATING BIBLICAL CONTRADICTIONS

—w—

I spent considerable time preparing to launch a full-blown investigation of the Bible. I would seek the best evidence available to determine whether the Bible was accurate and reliable, or filled with errors and contradictions. By chance, I met an atheist and Bible critic named Frankie in a mall bookstore. He saw me browsing through some books about the Bible, and we struck up a conversation. When I explained to him what I was trying to accomplish, he said he could help end my investigation in "short order." I obviously was interested in what he had to say. Any kind of shortcut to this project would be appreciated.

Frankie told me he had proof the Bible was full of contradictions and errors from an inside source, namely the Bible itself. My interest was peaked. If I could show numerous errors and contradictions in the Bible, then the case would be as good as closed. How can a book be accurate and inspired by the "almighty" God, yet still contain contradictions and errors? This could be some very damaging evidence against Christianity. Unprepared to take notes, I borrowed paper and pencil from the cashier. We found a comfortable place to sit, and he began showing me the problems in the Bible. After about two hours, I was armed with numerous contradictions and errors. It appeared that my expert witness had come through.

When I got home, I borrowed Denise's Bible and went through it to verify the passages Frankie had cited. After some time, I was able to find every contradiction he had pointed out. Now I was armed to do battle with a Bible expert, and maybe catch him or her off guard. This was going to be interesting. I will admit I was back to having a bias against the Bible, but now felt I had evidence to support my position. I couldn't wait to see how opposing "counsel" was going to handle this very incriminating evidence.

My next exchange with the same theologian went something like this:

I began the discussion, "Thanks for taking the time to see me again and so soon after my last visit. As I mentioned on the phone, there are some Biblical contradictions I would like to have you address if you don't mind?"

He leaned forward and commented, "I enjoyed our last discussion. I'm sure I will enjoy this one as well. You ask insightful questions, which helps keep me on my toes. I studied apologetics in seminary. It's easy to loose your edge if you aren't challenged. So go ahead and I will try my best to give you an answer. Not that I have them all."

I thought about his response for a moment. "Before I get started, what is apologetics?"

He leaned back in his chair with a pained expression on his face. "Sorry, I guess I did it again, using words that most in the lay community wouldn't understand. In theology, apologetics is simply a study that allows one to defend Christianity through logic and facts, with minimal dependence on accepting a belief based solely on faith."

"Okay, well that's good. I've come here looking for some concrete evidence related to the reliability of the Bible. However, I would first like to know how you reconcile and explain all the contradictions in the Bible?"

My statement elicited a slight smile from him. "That's a good question that first necessitates defining the word contradiction. A contradiction is when something claims to be both an 'x' and not an 'x' at the same time. In other words, you couldn't have been physically born in both Oakland and Los Angeles. That is impossible. If a document stated that you were born in Oakland on September 4, 1950 and another said you were born in Los Angeles on Sept 4, 1950, there would be a contradiction. One would be in error and thus untrue. Do you agree?"

I pondered that for a moment. "Yes, I do agree. I also agree with your definition of contradiction. By the way, you were kind to use 1950 as my birth year, but were off by seven years. Don't get a side job in a carnival guessing ages. You'll starve."

He laughed. "Good advice. I'm not gifted enough to work in a carnival. I understand from our mutual friend that you were once a 'carnie' working the baseball toss game."

"Dan's a big gossip, however he's right. That was a long time ago when I was in my teens."

With a very serious look he asked, "This is off the topic, but are the games fixed?"

Now I laughed. "I think today they are fairly well policed, but not in those days. In the baseball throw, two of the three bottles were leaded. I generally put them on the bottom, which made it almost impossible to knock them off the tire. When I had a large crowd around, I placed a leaded bottle on top. The idea was to get a winner and lose a teddy bear. That would sucker others into playing, at which time I placed the two leaded bottles on the bottom again. Enough of that. Let's get back to our discussion if you don't mind."

He paused. "Okay, but at one of these meetings I'd like to interview you about your experiences. Let's see. Where were we?"

I responded, "You had just defined the word contradiction. I believe I can point out a number of contradictions in your Bible. If that's true, then I would conclude that the Bible contains errors and therefore not reliable. Would you agree?"

"If you can show true errors, then I would concur with your conclusion. However, I don't believe the Bible contains contradictions. Keep in mind that according to the rules of literary criticism, one is obliged to give the benefit of the doubt to the literature and not to the critic, unless contradictions or inaccuracies can be proven."

I conceded, "That seems to be a fair rule. However, I do believe I can show you contradictions in the Bible that can't be defended."

"Okay, let's have them."

I leaned forward in anticipation. "In the Gospel of Luke, Jesus predicted that the generation he was addressing would live to see his return to earth as the second coming. He said and I quote, 'Truly, I say to you, this generation will not pass away before these things occur.' However, that generation did pass away and you Christians are still waiting almost 2,000 years later. Was this so-called Son of God wrong in his prophecy or was he misquoted?"

He answered immediately. "Neither. Jesus was referring to the generation that would be alive at the beginning of the events signaling the end times and his return. When Jesus used the words, *these things,* he was referring to earthquakes, plagues, nation against nation, etc. that were yet to come. The generation that witnessed the beginning of these signs would still be alive at the end. In Mark, Jesus is quoted as referring to these signs as '… merely the beginning of birth pangs.' That generation witnessing the 'birth pangs' would be present at the delivery of the promise."

Disappointed that he had a plausible answer, I continued. "Very good! This is going to be interesting. How about this one? The Gospels of Matthew, Luke, and John all give different accounts of how many angels there were at Jesus' tomb. Matthew describes only one angel, while Luke describes two, and John doesn't say anything about angels being present. That, my friend, is a definite contradiction. They all can't be right.

Remember your words, that it can't be an 'x' and 'non x' at the same time. How do you defend this obvious disagreement among these New Testament writers?"

He paused a moment, and I felt I had him stumped. Then confidently he answered, "I disagree with your conclusion. This was simply different accounts of the same event from three different views. Matthew didn't say there was only one angel and John didn't say there were no angels. In fact, John gives a much abbreviated version of this event. Varying descriptions of the same event are not contradictions. Actually, they tend to add credibility to the accounts showing that the witnesses didn't conspire together when writing about Jesus. It also adds credibility since witnesses never describe the same event in the exact same manner. I'm surprised as a highly skilled and trained investigator you didn't pick up on that. I would think that would have been obvious to you."

Uh oh! He had me on that one. I had to admit that was a sound answer. I sheepishly responded, "Okay, you're right. I guess I was too interested in proving the Bible wrong. I'm embarrassed that I didn't pick up on that possibility. Your response negates a large number of examples I was going to use to point out what I thought were contradictions. You took away most of my ammunition."

Trying to make me feel better he further explained, "Don't feel too bad. So-called learned Bible critics cite the same type of examples to disprove the Bible. Since this is their most common attack, I would like to provide you with a modern day illustration if you don't mind."

I nodded. "No, go ahead. I owe you that."

He continued. "Assume you saw the Sheriff and Chief of Police at a café, and told a friend that you saw the two of them together. Later you were talking to another friend and told that individual that you ran into the Sheriff at a cafe. Is that a contradiction? Are you lying because you failed to include the Chief in relaying the story to the second friend? Of course not! You were relaying the event to two different people for what could be a variety of reasons. If you had told the second friend that you only saw the Sheriff at the café, and didn't see the Chief then you would be lying and making a contradictory statement. I know that you as an investigator would be very suspicious if two witnesses' accounts of the same crime were exactly the same in all details."

"You made your point well." With much less confidence than when the discussion started I continued. "I won't be using any more examples of that nature. I have some other examples that appear to be contradictions I would like to ask you about. For instance, explain how two different Gospels give two different times for when Jesus was hung on the cross? Mark writes it was the third hour when they crucified him. John writes it was about the sixth hour or three hours later when he was condemned and delivered to be crucified. One of these versions must be wrong. A three-hour time difference is substantial and a definite contradiction."

He shook his head in the affirmative and replied, "Yes, a three hour difference would surely be a contradiction. However, in all probability, John was using a different method of describing time than Mark. The

Romans calculated the day from midnight to midnight much like the military. To the Romans the sixth hour would have been 6 a.m. or 0600 hours, which is the time John says the trial ended. That would provide plenty of time for the activities that preceded the actual crucifixion to take place by 9 a.m. which is the time cited by Mark. Mark was using the Jewish method of calculating time. The Jewish day was from sunset to sunset divided into eight equal parts. The first morning watch in Jewish time was 6 a.m. to 9 a.m. in the morning. That would make nine in the morning, the third hour."

I lowered my head. "Very good! Another one for your side, but I'm not giving up yet. Let's try something in the book of Acts written by Luke. In Acts 9:7 it reads that the men with Paul at his conversion to Christianity, 'heard a voice.' Later in Acts 22:9 Luke quotes Paul saying, 'they heard not the voice of him that spoke to me.' This is definitely a contradiction and by the same author. Either they heard or they didn't. It can't be both. You can't have been born in Oakland and Los Angeles at the same time. I was feeling pretty confident with this one."

"The Greek text uses two different forms of the Greek verb *to hear*. The verb *hear* in Acts 9:7 simply expresses sounds being heard, but not whether the person understood those sounds. Like hearing a rock song, but not having a clue what is being said. In Acts 22:9 the word *hear* is the accusative form of the verb and describes hearing that could include understanding the spoken word. In Acts 22:9 Luke the author isn't saying they didn't hear certain sounds, but rather they didn't hear in such a way as to understand what was being said. Acts 9:7 and Acts 22:9 say the same thing. In Acts 22:9 they did not hear a sound they understood, and in Acts 9:7 they heard a sound but didn't understand it. The Greek language tends to have more descriptive words than our language. For instance, they have three words for love that all denote different types of love. We have one word, *love*."

I conceded. "You're good! I doubt that I'm going to be able to stump you, but can I try a few more? I want to be totally convinced this type of attack against the Bible doesn't work."

Confidently he replied, "Sure, use as many examples as you like. I want you to feel satisfied that you have exhausted this avenue of Biblical criticism. If you study apologetics, you'll come to realize that the Bible is the most criticized and persecuted book ever written. People for hundreds of years have tried to discredit the Bible. As far as I know, and from what I have read, none have been successful. However they keep trying."

Right about now, my "star witness" Frankie certainly didn't seem credible. It didn't appear his information was going to help me achieve the results I was hoping to reach. Nonetheless, I took another try and said, "Let's switch to the Old Testament. Maybe I'll do better there. I assume you agree with most Bible scholars that Moses wrote the first five books of the Old Testament?"

He nodded. "Your assumption is correct."

I continued. "Explain how he could have written the five books, when in the fifth one called Deuteronomy there are accounts of his death?"

He hesitated momentarily. "It would appear that you have me on this one, except for a common practice in those days. That practice involved placing an obituary at the end of the final work by a great author. In the case of Deuteronomy, it is believed Moses wrote the first 33 chapters, including his farewell address. It is believed that Joshua, who is mentioned in Chapter 34, wrote the last chapter which would be consistent with the practice of those times."

"You sure know apologetics. However, I'm going to try a few more times. Judges 5:25-27 relates that Jael killed Sisera while Sisera was drinking milk. Judges 4:21 states that Sisera was sleeping when killed by Jael, thus he could hardly be drinking milk. How do you account for the differences?"

He reached over to the table and picked up his leather bound Bible. "You may have me. This is a new one. Let me study the passages in the Bible for a minute."

"Sure. Take your time."

I watched him turn to the proper section of his Bible and study the passages. Then suddenly he grinned and I knew he had an answer. "Ah, here it is." He moved the Bible pages so I could view them. "Notice in the verses preceding Judges 4:21 that Sisera asked Jael for water but she gave him milk. She then covered him and subsequently killed him while he slept. Careful reading of Judges 5:25-27 doesn't say he was drinking milk, but rather she simply gave him milk prior to the time she drove a tent peg into Sisera's temple. There is no contradiction."

I proceeded with a few more examples of possible errors or contradictions in the Bible. They included the two different genealogy accounts of Jesus and the two different versions of how Judas died. The results were the same as the other examples. I finally decided to give up. I conceded that what appeared to be contradictions in the Bible could be logically explained by Biblical scholars.

"Isn't it curious that Bible critics try to grab even the smallest possible inconsistency to attempt to discredit the Book? Although they haven't been successful, they continue to try. Ask yourself if the same degree of scrutiny has been applied to any other book?"

"I really don't know enough to answer that right now. I can say that Frankie was sure these examples were enough to discredit the Bible. I guess he and others don't take the time to examine the other side. I'm sorry that I let this potential shortcut destroy my neutrality. I think you helped get me back on track as an unbiased investigator. Thanks!"

"You're very welcome. Good luck with the rest of your investigation. I hope you let me know the results. I must warn you that I will be praying for you to become a believer."

I laughed. "The horse race crowd would call that a long shot and I mean a real long shot. Don't put any money on it. You're better off to bet the Cubs will soon win a World Series."

Well, that was an interesting exchange. I felt a little embarrassed that I had been so taken in by Frankie. I would have liked to run into him again to see how he would react to the counter arguments to his so-called contradictions in the Bible. I never saw Frankie again. My investigation of the Bible continued. I began to realize this was going to be one of those long-term cases. I should never have let Denise con me into this project.

CHAPTER 10

INVESTIGATING THE MANUSCRIPTS

—〰—

The next step in my investigation was to do more reading about the Bible. It was time to focus on the issue of reliability. Can the book be trusted as historically accurate, or is it basically fiction written to justify a religious cult? I talked with some Christian friends who suggested a number of books they thought might be helpful. They included; *How to Understand the Bible*, *Know Why You Believe*, *Reason to Believe*, and *Evidence that Demands a Verdict*.

These books, along with additional reading material and a series of discussions, led to the discovery of some very interesting information. Again, for ease of reading, I will put this phase of my investigation into an interview format. Some of these discussions actually took place, while other information came from books. Unfortunately, I do not write well enough to separate and identify the information obtained from the books as opposed to the interviews. Remember, I'm a cop; not an author. I'm also not sure at this time,

I could differentiate between the two. If you want the references for this material, they can be found in Part Two. As my investigation continued, I interviewed another theologian. The discussion follows:

He was behind his desk when I entered his office. Standing at the doorway I said, "Thank you for agreeing to meet and explain why you consider the Bible accurate and reliable. I'm interested in any evidence you may be able to provide."

He got up from behind his desk and we shook hands. "Please come in and have a seat at the table. May I get you a cup of coffee?"

"No, I'm fine. When we spoke on the phone I explained my purpose."

He nodded. "Yes, I understand your position and the purpose of this interview. It will be my pleasure to try to present a case for the Bible. Please don't hesitate to interrupt if you don't understand, or want to challenge my point. Lively debate is healthy."

I smiled. "Let's begin! The Bible is a very old document that goes back before Christ. How on earth can anyone verify its accuracy or trustworthiness?"

With a thoughtful look he responded, "Good question! I think we should use the same method that is used to judge all documents of antiquity. Our entire history before the 19th century is based primarily on the written record. How can we be sure what we believe about the past is accurate? There is a study called historiography that helps us judge the reliability of historical documents. It is easier to apply when the writing in question was written in more recent times. However, this method is also used to test ancient works for accuracy. There are basically three tests that are used."

"What are those tests?"

He replied, "The bibliographical, internal evidence, and external evidence tests."

My ears perked up. "I like this already since two out of the three are presumed to be evidence. Finally, a term I'm familiar with!" I continued, "That's what I'm looking for, evidence. Let's start with the bibliographical first if that works for you?"

He agreed. "That's a good place to start. The bibliographical test examines how accurate the current manuscript is in relationship to the original writing. In other words are we reading substantially the same as how the ancient work was originally written? This test consists of three parts: 1) How many different manuscripts exist? 2) How close in time are the earliest manuscripts to the date of the original writing? 3) How accurate is the current translation compared to the earliest manuscript?

Let me try another way of summarizing the three parts of the bibliographical test.

The more manuscripts and the closer in time they are to the original writing, then the more trustworthy the document. Also, the fewer textual variations or differences between the manuscripts and the current document, the more reliable the current document."

I thought for a moment. "I think I understand the elements of this test. How does the Bible score in comparison to other historical documents?"

Without hesitation he answered, "In my opinion and that of other scholars, the Bible warrants an extremely high score and far exceeds all other documents of antiquity. In fact, it isn't even a contest with the other documents. You law enforcement officers would probably compare it to having an air tight case that would easily result in a guilty plea or verdict."

I grinned. "That's a lot of confidence on your part. Let's see if you can back it up with facts."

Confidently he replied, "Fine. Let's start with a work that most scholars tend to trust as reliable in relationship to the original document and what we now read. That would be Homer's *Iliad*. Are you familiar with this work?"

"Yes, in high school I once had to do a book report on the *Iliad*. With the help of my girlfriend and a classic comic book, I was able to obtain a decent grade. I actually enjoyed the story of the Trojan War."

He nodded. "It was written about 700 B.C. and was based on an actual war fought between Greece and the city of Troy. It's interesting to note that some critics claimed that Homer couldn't have written the *Iliad*, since written language hadn't been discovered at that time. That's the same argument they use against Moses having written the first five books of the Bible. As is often the case, archeology has proven the critics wrong."

Curiously I asked, "Why do you bring up the *Iliad*?"

"I'm sorry I got off track. The reason I mention this virtually undisputed ancient writing is because the tests show that there were over 600 copies of manuscripts, and the earliest was within 300 to 500 years of the original writing. Compared to other works like Aristotle's writings and Caesar's *Gallic Wars*, the *Iliad* wins hand down. Aristotle's work has only about 50 copies with approximately a 1,300-year time span. Caesar's *Gallic Wars* has only about 10 copies with approximately a 1,000-year time span. However, compared to the Bible, the *Iliad* never leaves the starting block. The New Testament has over 5,000 copies of manuscripts, with the earliest being as close as 25 to 85 years of the original writing."

"That's pretty impressive. Are there any ancient works that come close?"

"The closest we can determine is the *Iliad*."

I conceded, "Okay that gives the Bible a point, but still a long way from proving its reliability. You said there were three parts to the bibliographical tests. What is the third and how does the Bible score? It had something to do with differences."

"We are talking about the number of differences in what we read compared to the earliest manuscripts. We call that the corruption rate. The New Testament has less than one half of one percent corruption rate, which is only 400 words out of over 184,000."

I was surprised. "That's really amazing. I would have guessed at least 25%. Are there any other old books or documents that have a low rate? What is the rate for the *Iliad*?"

He paused a moment. "The *Iliad* has a 5% error rate and the *Mahabharata* or History of India has a 10% error rate. That's really not too bad, but substantially more than the New Testament. The Bible is truly unique and stands alone using the bibliographical test. Don't you agree?"

Reluctantly I replied, "I admit I'm impressed that the New Testament scored so high. Can you tell me what the differences are in the 400 corrupted words?"

Without hesitation he explained, "Yes, they are mostly errors in either style or spelling. None are substantial variations that affect the meaning of what is being conveyed. In fact, the noted authority on New Testament textual criticism, Sir Frederic Kenyon stated, 'No fundamental doctrine of the Christian faith rests on disputed reading ... It cannot be too strongly asserted that in substance the text of the Bible is certain. Especially is this the case with the New Testament ...' Dr Gleason Archer of Trinity Divinity School in answer to an inquiry responded, 'A careful study of the variants of the various earliest manuscripts reveals that none of them affects a single doctrine of Scripture ...' Critics of the Bible have been unable to rebut this fact."

"Anything else before we go on to the other tests?"

He leaned forward in his chair. "As a matter of fact there is. We have evidence for the New Testament that doesn't exist for other ancient works. The New Testament was quoted so often by early church leaders that it can be reconstructed from their writings. There were over 36,000 quotations prior to A. D. 325. These quotations confirm that what we are reading today is substantially the same as was written over 2,000 years ago."

I shook my head. "You really know this subject. I see that I came to the right place. However, all this tells us is that the New Testament we read today is about the same as when it was written. That's the only conclusion that can be drawn from the bibliographical test. That doesn't prove what was written is accurate or reliable."

He agreed. "You are absolutely correct, but we still have two other parts of historiography."

I interrupted him. "Before you go on to the other two, you really haven't said much about the Old Testament. Are we leaving it out? I thought it was part or about half of the entire Bible. How does it fare when tested?"

"Good question and observation on your part. The number of manuscripts and their proximity to the original writings was similar to other ancient works. For instance, like Caesar's *Gallic Wars* the oldest manuscript was about A.D. 900; approximately a 1300-year gap from when it was written. That was before 1947 when the Dead Sea Scrolls were discovered. Do you know about the scrolls?"

"I know that a shepherd boy found some ancient scrolls in a cave in Israel, and Christians were very excited about the discovery. Other than that, I didn't pay much attention to exactly what was found."

"Among other documents they found scrolls written 100 years before the birth of Christ. The scrolls included two complete copies of Isaiah that prove to be 95% identical word for word to what we read today. The differences for the most part consisted of slips of the pen and misspellings. For instance, of the 166 words in Isaiah Chapter 53, only seventeen letters were in question. Ten of these were misspellings and four were only minor style changes. The remaining three comprise the word 'light' added to verse 11 that doesn't affect the meaning. That's pretty amazing. What would you have bet the odds were for those results after 2,000 years?"

I smiled. "About the same as the Chicago Cubs wining the World Series next year. It's definitely a bet I wouldn't have taken."

He continued. "By the way, fragments of Deuteronomy and Samuel show no differences."

I found myself again conceding. "I'll give this one to your Bible. The evidence is overwhelming. You've given me a lot of information to digest. I would like to take some time to organize my notes, and make sure they are accurate by reviewing them with you. Do you mind if we take a break?"

He shook his head. "No, not at all. I have a number of phone calls to make. You can use the office across the hall. No one will bother you. When you are ready to continue just come back in. We can go over your notes, then discuss the other tests. There's water and coffee in the kitchen."

"Thanks. I really appreciate your time. I think I will take a cup of coffee. Can I get you one?"

"No, but I will take a glass of ice water if you don't mind. I appreciate your gratitude but it's my pleasure. I will be interested in the results of your investigation."

I got his water and my coffee, then went across the hall to a small office. I sat at an old metal desk and began putting my notes into a report format. He gave me a lot of information in a short period of time.

I had not known what to expect from this interview. I certainly had gathered more information than I had anticipated, and there were still two tests to go. This was interesting but a long way from proving Christianity. I made a mental note to ask him about the different translations of the Bible. Which one was accurate? If one was accurate, then why are there other translations? It seems as though there should only be one.

CHAPTER 11

THE INTERNAL
EVIDENCE TEST

—ᨓ—

When I returned to his office about fifteen minutes later, we went over my notes to make sure my information was accurate. He seemed quite impressed. I had at least scored points on my note-taking ability. As an investigator, I had a lot of practice recording what others reported. I would have been embarrassed if my notes were inaccurate. It was bad enough that my attack with those so-called contradictions had totally bombed. We sat down at the rounded table and continued our discussion.

I started. "Before we proceed with the other two tests, I would like to ask you about the different versions of the Bible."

He replied, "I was wondering if that issue would come up. What do you want to know?"

"Since there is more than one version of the Bible, how can they all be correct?"

He leaned back in his chair. "There are many different versions of the Bible. They are all based on the earliest manuscripts. The different versions were primarily developed for style and readability. Some of the more popular ones include; *King James Version, New American Standard Bible, New International Version*, and *New Living Translation*. The *King James Version* was written in old English and is considered by many as an example of classical use of that language. Most people in our country find it difficult to read and understand. The *New Living Translation* is easy to read and uses simple everyday language. The *New International Version* and *New American Standard Bible* are somewhere in-between. In general terms, the content and meaning of the various translations are similar. However, a person can always research the earliest versions or refer to commentaries. The commentaries often give the original word, the meaning of the verses, the context within which it was written, and some cultural background."

He continued. "The easiest way to explain the different versions is that most try to stick as close as possible to the original meaning, but were developed for a particular style and/or ease of reading and understanding. The Greek language has many more words to relay a meaning than English. Greeks have at least three words for love, whereas we only have one. According to the best selling book, *The Purpose Driven Life*, the Bible was written using over eleven thousand Hebrew and Greek words for which we use only about six thousand words. I hope that adequately answered your question."

I nodded. "Yes. Thanks. Which version of the Bible do you prefer?"

"I tend to lean toward either the New International or New American. My experience is that they tend to be closer to the original Greek or Hebrew words found in early manuscripts, yet are understandable. Although sometimes I will use the Living Bible because of it's more modern use of our everyday language. I also use commentaries on a regular basis to help better understand what I'm reading."

I was anxious to try to cover the other two tests at this meeting. "Let's move on to the other two tests used to prove the reliability of the Bible. I seem to remember the second one was the internal test. What does that consist of?"

"The internal evidence test consists of three parts. The first consideration is the primary source of the information. Much like in criminal law, the best source is an eyewitness to the recorded event. Someone who receives the information directly from an eyewitness is the next best source. The further down the chain from an eyewitness that the information is received, then the less credible it is considered."

He continued. "The second part is to determine how close the primary source was in relationship to the time and geography of the recorded event. The closer in time and geography, the more reliable. Some events weren't recorded until the story was passed down over generations. This test also gives preference to an eyewitness. The last part of the internal test is to determine whether persons who lived at the same time and place as the event were still living when it was documented. These would be people who could have refuted what was written."

I asked, "How does the Bible rate when these tests are applied?"

"Extremely well, particularly in regard to the New Testament. We have so much more information to examine than we do with the Old Testament. But, don't take that to mean the Old Testament is unreliable"

"How many of the authors of the New Testament were eye witnesses?"

"There are eight authors of the New Testament books. Five of them were eyewitnesses to the events and words they recorded. The other three obtained their information directly from eyewitnesses. All of the authors lived at the same time and geographic location as the recorded events. They also completed their gospels and letters when people were still living who could have refuted what they recorded. Many, such as the Romans and especially the Jewish leaders, had good reason to try to dispute their writings. Researchers haven't been able to locate documents from that time that actually refute or attempts to refute what was written. I would give the New Testament another A+."

I acknowledged, "From an investigators stand point that is pretty good evidence. The testimony of eyewitnesses is excellent evidence as long as they can't be impeached. Apparently most of the New Testament writers were eyewitnesses who weren't impeached or shown to have perjured themselves. However, I want to personally review what they testified about, and try to determine if they made any impeachable statements."

He had a big grin on his face. "That's a great prelude into the third and final test which can be used to impeach a writer's testimony. However, I want to cover one other point under the internal evidence test. This point should be especially meaningful to you as a criminal investigator."

Curiously I asked, "What point is that?"

He responded, "You will agree that the writers of the New Testament were all followers of Jesus?"

"As far as I know."

He then asked, "Wouldn't you find it meaningful in regard to credibility, if the writers recorded both favorable and unfavorable information about their leaders?"

"Yes." I replied, "A good witness does not leave anything out, even unfavorable information. That in itself makes the witness more believable. Yes, I would find that compelling!"

He nodded. "Good! The Bible writers did not conceal incidents that portrayed their leaders unfavorably. If they were making up these stories or weren't concerned about the truth, they could have omitted the unfavorable events and behavior in their writings. Some of these included but certainly are not limited to; the weaknesses and sins of Old Testament heroes, Peter's denial of Jesus, the apostles competing for higher places in heaven, Jesus' stress resulting in sweating blood, the apostles going into hiding because of fear, Jesus' anger in the Temple, Jesus' despair in the garden and on the cross, and Thomas' doubting that Jesus had risen from the grave. For me one of the most compelling was that the Gospel writers were willing to admit that women were the first witnesses to the risen Christ. During that time in the Jewish culture, women were considered unreliable witnesses. In fact, women were possessions and generally treated like property by Jewish men, except for a few like Jesus and his followers."

I leaned forward in my chair. "That's an excellent point in favor of the Biblical writers. Those are very interesting observations that I'll want to explore more deeply, especially regarding the Old Testament heroes and their faults. Can we move on to the last test before we run out of time?"

CHAPTER 12

THE EXTERNAL EVIDENCE TEST

—⁓—

He agreed to move on. "That would be the external evidence test. This examination should be most interesting to you. It tends to address your question about impeaching the testimony of the Bible authors. The test examines whether or not there is independent historical material that confirms or refutes the tested document. In other words, what outside sources, if any, substantiate the accuracy and reliability of the document?"

"This should be good!" I commented.

He began, "There are a number of outside sources that confirm the reliability and trustworthiness of the Bible. For instance, many of the apostles and early religious leaders testified to the accuracy of Scripture."

I interrupted. "I wouldn't consider them outside sources. Don't you think they have a built-in bias? Their faith was largely built on what later became the Bible."

He responded, "I think that should be taken into consideration when you examine their testimony. I don't think you should automatically judge them to be liars simply because they were followers of Christ. Many of these ethical men were martyred for their strong convictions."

I shot back. "Dying for a belief doesn't make it true. Just look at the mass suicide of the Jim Jones religious cult or the kamikaze pilots in World War II."

He leaned back in his chair. "You're right, but the circumstance, especially with the apostles, was quite different. These men were eyewitnesses to the events and knew with certainty whether or not they were true. This wasn't something that so-called leaders used to convince or manipulate them. These men knew beyond a shadow of doubt whether Jesus appeared to them after his death. They knew that the miracles actually happened. They were eyewitnesses. Almost all of them submitted to terrible deaths for what they knew to be the truth. If they died for what they knew were lies, they were crazy fools. There is absolutely no evidence to support an insanity theory. In fact, the evidence demonstrates that these men where of sound mind and lived by high ethical standards. Consider also that the other religious leaders knew some of the apostles and were familiar with many of the events recorded."

I conceded. "Good point. You were relating about the early Church leaders before you were so rudely interrupted."

"Okay. Let's continue. Papias, the Bishop of Heirapolis wrote about John, Mark, and Matthew in positive terms. He said that Mark accompanied Peter and accurately recorded what Peter relayed to him. Irenaeus, the Bishop of Lyons wrote, 'So firm is the ground, which these Gospels rest that the very heretics themselves bare witness to them ....' There were many other early Church leaders who wrote similar things about the Bible and its writers."

As he paused a moment I interjected, "What about non-religious leaders from that time?"

"Good question. There were a number of non-believers who wrote about the people or events in the Bible. Josephus, the renowned Jewish historian wrote about John the Baptist. He also wrote about Jesus, his amazing feats, his following, and crucifixion. Suetonius, the Roman historian wrote briefly about Chrestus (Christ), as did the Samaritan historian Thallus. He explained away the darkness that occurred when Jesus died as an eclipse of the sun. There were others also."

"Is that all there is to the external evidence test?"

He smiled. "Oh gracious no! That's just the warm up. The next significant aspect of the test is to determine if archaeology supports or contradicts the Bible."

"What does your research show?"

He continued. "Archaeology is a major source in demonstrating that the Bible is a trustworthy document. Critics over hundreds of years have repeatedly tried to disprove the Bible. They felt that some of the Biblical information had been discredited. They pointed out situations where no other source except the Bible mentioned some of the people, places, and events described. That was sufficient for them to determine that the Bible was not trustworthy. Over time the study of archaeology has repeatedly shown these critics to be wrong. Renowned Jewish archaeologist Nelson Glueck wrote, 'It may be stated categorically that no archaeological discovery has ever controverted a Biblical reference.' Archaeologist Joseph Freeman wrote, 'Archaeology has confirmed countless passages which have been rejected by critics as unhistorical or contradictory to known fact.'"

"Can you give me some examples?" I asked.

After taking a drink of water, he answered, "Sure! Keep in mind there are many books written about archaeology supporting the Bible. I'll give you a few examples. For instance, critics were positive, contrary to what the Old Testament said, that there was no Hittite civilization at the time of Abraham. That charge lasted only until archaeological finds confirmed that not only did the Hittite civilization exist, but did so during the time of Abraham. Critics said that the Bible's account of Nebuchadnezzar's humble family birth was inaccurate. They assumed he was of royal birth. After all, no one could become king from a non-royal family. Archaeologist discovered an inscription by his father, Nabopolassar, which revealed the Bible was correct. The inscription said that Babylon's greatest king was, 'the son of a nobody' indicating non-royal birth. Another example was when critics discounted Abraham's victory over the Mesopotamian kings and the five cities that were mentioned. They claimed this account was fictional since no other historical document had ever mentioned the victory or the five cities. The discovery of the Eble Tablets in the 1960's lists all five cities, and helped to confirm the Old Testament account related to the region. Lastly, the critics stated categorically that Moses could not have been the author of the first five books of the Old Testament. They claimed that written language hadn't been discovered at the time of Moses. The Black Stele containing the Laws of Hammurabi was subsequently discovered, and archaeologist confirmed that it pre-dated Moses by three centuries. As a matter of fact, the Bible mentions numerous places, events, and individuals, yet not one single piece of archeology has ever refuted the Bible."

I had to admit that I was impressed. "Wow! You really do know this subject matter. I noticed however that all of the examples came from the Old Testament. What about the New Testament? Are there any similar illustrations?"

He nodded. "Yes, there are many parallel instances from the New Testament. Would you like me to cover a few?"

"Yes. I want to make sure my investigation is thorough. Just give me two or three more examples."

He agreed. "One of the greatest archaeologists, who ever lived, Sir William Ramsey, set out to dispute Luke's accounts in the Book of Acts. He admits that he entered his investigation with a prejudice against the historian, Luke. After thirty years of study he wrote, 'Luke is a historian of the first rank, not merely are his statements of fact trustworthy … this author should be placed along with the greatest of historians.' He continued, 'Luke's history is unsurpassed in respect of its trustworthiness.' In another case, critics refuted the New Testament's claim that there was a census, or that Quirinius was Governor of Syria around the time that Jesus was born. Archaeologists discovered an inscription in Antioch that confirmed that Quirinius was governor at the time Jesus was born. They also discovered proof that the Romans had a census every fourteen years. An ancient document concerning the Roman Empire found in Egypt read, ' because of the approaching census it is necessary that all those residing for any cause away from their homes ... prepare to return to their own governments in order that they may complete the family registration of the enrollment ....' There are many more examples, but you said a few would suffice for your purposes."

I nodded my head affirmatively. "Yes. I'm satisfied with the examples. My head is spinning with all the information you provided. Is that it for the third test?"

"No, there is one more part which I consider the most compelling evidence for the authenticity of the Bible."

"Can we take a short break before we proceed? I want to go over my notes to make sure I'm not missing anything."

"Your call. You can stay here. I need to stretch my legs. How much time do you want?"

"How about fifteen minutes?"

"That's perfect. It takes me about that long to walk around the grounds."

He left his office and went outside. I went into the kitchen and poured another cup of coffee. I returned to his office and proceeded to study my notes. They were better than I expected. Although, I was sure that at some point, I would have to call him to clarify some of what he presented. The fifteen minutes passed quickly.

EXAMINING BIBLICAL PROPHECIES

—ɯ—

Almost to the minute, he returned to the office and asked, "Do you need more time or are you ready to continue?"

I looked up at him standing in the doorway. "No. I'm fine. Let's continue!"

He sat in his chair and asked about my notes. I told him they seemed complete, but I may have to call him later when I reviewed them in more detail. He agreed and then asked, "Are you ready for the last part of the external evidence test?"

"Yes, definitely! I can't imagine what's left that you consider the most compelling evidence in support of the Bible. I thought about that during the break and couldn't come up with an answer. Actually, I have been waiting in anticipation."

"Part three of the external test has to do with prophecies. I believe this will definitely put you over the edge and convince you beyond a reasonable doubt. Are you familiar with prophecies?"

I looked directly at him with an expression of skepticism. "I know what prophecies are, but I'm only vaguely familiar with any specifics or how they support the Bible. You seem awfully sure of yourself. I'm going to hate to disappoint you when this doesn't put me over the edge."

He laughed. "Now! Now! Please try to stay objective. Remember, you're a professional member of our elite law enforcement community. Try to rid yourself of any bias."

I agreed. "Okay. Your point is well taken. Tell me about prophecies and how they support the Bible."

He seemed almost excited to respond. "Actually, prophecy is the oral or written message of God proclaimed by a prophet who was divinely inspired. The predictive element was frequently part of the content of the prophet's message. Webster's Dictionary defines prophecy as, 'inspired utterance of divine will and purpose; a prediction of something to come.' Prophecy is not fortunetelling, soothsaying, or clairvoyance. There is no guesswork. Unlike other forecasting measures, the predictive element of prophecy must occur and be accurate. The reason why this is so important is that man has been unable to predict specific events in the distant future with any degree of reliability or consistency. That is not the case with Bible prophecies."

"What are some examples of these unique prophecies?"

He answered, "Let's start with the Old Testament. The prophet Ezekiel's ministry was to the Jews exiled to Babylonian from 592 to 570 B.C. He wrote specifically about the fate of the city of Tyre before it occurred. He said that King Nebuchadnezzar would destroy the mainland of the city. He continued that subsequently many nations would rise up against the city and that eventually it would be totally destroyed. Ezekiel wrote that Tyre will become, '… a bare rock; you will be a place for the spreading of nets. You will be built no more ….'"

To say I was intrigued was an understatement. "So what specifically happened and how long after the prediction?"

With confidence he answered, "Three years after the prophecy, Tyre's mainland was attacked by King Nebuchadnezzar and after thirteen years the old mainland city was destroyed. Most of the people fled to an island just off the coast and re-established the city of Tyre. The city was attacked over the next 1800 years until finally it was destroyed by the Muslims in A.D. 1291. It was never rebuilt on the original spot. That area became a bare rock used by fishermen to spread their nets to dry. Even today, fishermen still use that exact place to dry their nets."

I sat back in my chair amazed. "Wow! That's a little eerie. Any more examples like that one?"

"Yes, the Bible is filled with those kinds of prophecies. Remember, the Bible is a book inspired by God. If you believed that, the prophecies wouldn't seem so weird, eerie, or spooky. How else can you explain the prophecies and their reliability? Is it due to chance? I don't think so. Pete Stoner, a professor of mathematics, estimates that there was only one chance in 75 million that all the predictions about Tyre could come true. Let's continue so you realize that Ezekiel wasn't unique in terms of Biblical prophecy."

He continued. "The great prophet Isaiah wrote in about 700 B.C. that a man specifically named Cyrus would build Jerusalem and lay the foundation for the temple. Those living at that time who heard this prophecy must have thought that Isaiah had lost his mind. You see, at that time Jerusalem was fully built and the temple was standing. However, approximately one hundred years later in, 586 B.C., King Nebuchadnezzar destroyed the city and temple. Fifty years later the Persians conquered Jerusalem. The Persian king named - now get this - Cyrus gave a decree to rebuild the city and the temple. That was about 160 years after Isaiah wrote down the prophecy. Is this chance or divine intervention? If chance, what are the odds? I would be more confident betting the Cubs will win the World Series for the next five consecutive years. In fact, someone calculated the odds as one in ten to the 39th for just seven specific Old Testament prophecies being fulfilled."

He took a pen out of his shirt pocket and tore off a piece of paper from a tablet lying on the table. He then proceeded to write down the following: 1 in 1,000,000,000,000,000,000,000,000,000,000,000,000,000. "That my friend is the probability of just those seven predictions coming true."

Needless to say I felt a little overwhelmed. "Does the New Testament play into the prophecies at all?"

He gave that little grin again and I knew he was ready. "Funny you should ask."

I interrupted. "You're enjoying this, aren't you? Go ahead and let me have it."

He began. "I have to admit that I have enjoyed watching your expressions and body language. We are close to the conclusion of the third test."

"Good! No offense, but I'll need a stiff drink after this session."

"No offense taken, but I would prefer you let me take you to dinner. I'd like to know more about your background and work as an undercover agent. You happen to be the first one I've met."

"Sounds like a deal. Let's finish up. I'm a little hungry and suffering from information overload."

He continued with more comments about New Testament prophecies. "Theologians cite between 200 and 300 Old Testament prophecies that were fulfilled hundreds of years later in the New Testament. Some appear a little vague for me to totally accept.

Like you, I tend to be a skeptic. I'm willing to acknowledge that there are at least sixty messianic prophecies that actually were fulfilled in the person of Jesus Christ."

I questioned him. "Messianic means what?"

He answered, "It is defined as relating to the Messiah; the Savior sent by God to redeem mankind. These particular prophecies specifically predicted things that would be fulfilled in the one true Messiah. Does that answer your question?"

"Yes. Thanks!"

He continued. "I'm not going to take the time to cover all sixty right now. It isn't necessary and would probably be overkill, as well as overload. In the science of criminology, there are certain things considered irrefutable evidence in a court of law, such as fingerprints. With fingerprints, you only need eight matches of whorls, arches and loops on one finger to prove that the fingerprint belongs to a particular suspect. Thus it should only require eight non-refutable Old Testament prophecies fulfilled hundreds of years later to convict the Bible of being accurate and trustworthy."

We laughed together at his obvious knowledge of fingerprints, something so closely related to law enforcement and not theology. "Are you showing off?" I asked.

"Why that would be prideful and I'm a man of the cloth," He replied.

When we finally gained our composure this charming man of the cloth continued.

He took out his pen, grabbed another piece of paper, and began to write a list as he talked. "Various Old Testament prophets predicted that among other things the
Messiah would be:

1. Preceded by a messenger
2. Born in Bethlehem
3. Born of a virgin
4. His ministry would be in Galilee
5. He would perform miracles
6. Ride as a king mounted on a donkey
7. He will be betrayed by a friend
8. He will be betrayed for 30 pieces of silver
9. His hands and feet would be pierced

10. They would cast lots for His garments
11. He would be offered gall or vinegar
12. He would cry out forsaken
13. No bones would be broken
14. His side would be pierced."

He stopped and pointed to his list. "Jesus Christ fulfilled each and every one of those prophecies about the Messiah. They were made at a time, before crucifixion was ever used or even known about. I can show you the verse or verses in the Old Testament for each prophecy, and where in the New Testament Jesus fulfilled all fourteen."

I responded, "That won't be necessary for the purposes of this interview. If you wouldn't mind, I would like to get a copy of your Bible citations so I can review them at a later time."

He replied, "Not at all. I'll loan you a book with all that I mentioned and many more, so you can confirm them for yourself."

"Thanks. May I ask why your list contains fourteen examples rather than only eight?"

"I purposely went beyond the necessary eight matches required simply to emphasize my point. I think with everything presented, you could conclude beyond a reasonable doubt that the Bible is a one-of-a-kind document that is trustworthy and accurate."

"The case you presented is certainly overwhelming. I need time to think about the evidence and complete more research. I'm not quite ready to ask a jury to convict the Bible of being trustworthy and accurate. Although, the evidence right now seems to favor the Bible."

I thought to myself, "How could that be?" I felt conflicted and stressed. This is not what I had expected to find. Oh sure, I always imagined that I would find some bits and pieces of minor circumstantial evidence to support the Bible. But I never expected anything like this. There was such overwhelming evidence that I couldn't refute. This whole investigation had my mind spinning. In fact, I had a headache, which was rare for me. I then asked, "Is that it?"

He asked to make one last point and I agreed. "These fourteen prophecies were fulfilled 500 - 700 years after they were written down. The chance of just eight being fulfilled in one man is 1 in 10 to the 17th. That would be one followed by sixteen zeros. Peter Stoner, the mathematics professor I mentioned before, uses an illustration to demonstrate this probability. He says the odds of eight prophecies coming true in one person are the same odds of laying silver dollars two feet deep across the entire State of Texas. The next step would be to mark just one silver dollar somewhere in this pile that covers 266,874 square miles. Then blindfold a man and ask him to travel around the state and pick out the marked silver dollar somewhere in Texas."

He looked intently at me. "What are the odds of that happening? The same as Jesus Christ fulfilling eight of the Old Testament prophecies about the Messiah. Chance or Divine intervention? I really don't know how anyone could conclude that the

Bible is unreliable or inaccurate. Are you ready to relax and go to dinner?"

Relieved I responded, "Yes! I'm on empty. I'm not sure I could take in any more information. You remind me of a machine gun firing and hitting the target with each round. I'll have to check the target to see if there are any misses."

He laughed. "Good analogy. I must warn you that in the Marines I was a sharpshooter. Don't expect to find any misses. How about Fulton's Prime Rib in Old Sacramento?"

"Sounds great. Let's go!"

CHAPTER 14

PROMOTION AND RELOCATION

—⁓—

I'm going to digress a bit to the time prior to my investigation of Christianity. Upon completing my assignment at the DOJ Advanced Training Center in 1974, I was asked by Chief Bob Jensen to establish and supervise the Department's Special Operations Unit. This select team was created to target organized crime. I worked that assignment for eighteen months until a new administration eliminated the unit. I then developed and managed a project called the Sacramento Heroin Impact Program. After a year, this highly touted and successful program was turned over to local law enforcement. The new Assistant Chief felt it was inappropriate for a state agency. He wanted the California Bureau of Narcotics Enforcement to target major drug suppliers. I was reassigned to supervise a crew of drug enforcement agents targeting large-scale drug dealers and organizations. It was at the end of this assignment, in late 1979, that I began my investigation of Christianity.

Shortly thereafter, I was asked to set up and command a multi-agency task force in Placer County, California called the Placer Law Enforcement Agencies Special Investigation Unit. This great assignment only lasted a year because I was promoted.

One afternoon in late fall 1980, I received a telephone call from Chief Steve Helsley. He told me that I had been selected for promotion to special-agent-in-charge. The Chief explained that there were two openings, and I could select the one I wanted. It was either the San Francisco or the Fresno office. I had twenty-four hours to decide. I left work early and drove home to discuss this decision with Denise. The drive from Auburn, the headquarters of the task force, to Rancho Cordova where we lived, took about forty-five minutes. I began weighing the pros and cons for both locations. I had known this promotion was a possibility, so I already did some advanced research.

Personally I would rather manage the San Francisco office. It was larger and I knew the area, having worked there quite often. I felt San Francisco would be more challenging and exciting. There were some big cases to be made. That office covered the territory from a little north of San Jose along the coast to the Oregon border. It included Oakland, Richmond, the Napa Valley, and an area called the Emerald Triangle because of the large number of marijuana gardens. I knew it was expensive to live in the Bay area, and the cost of housing was at least double that of Sacramento. I also wasn't thrilled with the liberal bent to Bay Area politics and values.

The Fresno office covered the territory from Merced down to Bakersfield, which was called the San Joaquin Valley. The area is well known for its agriculture. The most positive aspect of Fresno was its relatively low cost of living. This afford-ability would allow us to live in a nice neighborhood without a long commute and, therefore, be better for the family. Terri would be going to college the following year so money was important. The Valley was also more conservative. I knew very little about the Fresno office personnel or their productivity. I had only worked with them on one case.

When I pulled up to the house after my commute, Denise met me at the door. Terri and Tom were still in school. Terri was a senior at St. Francis High School and Tom was in seventh grade at St. John Vianney School. It was a warm and sunny fall day so we sat outside on the patio to talk. I must have gone through a gallon of sweet tea (Southern influence). Denise and I discussed the promotion and relocation for about three hours.

She wasn't much help. She kept saying that she was fine with either location and it was up to me to decide. Denise was confident we could make it work wherever we lived.

The next day I called the Chief and told him I would take the Fresno office. He chuckled on the phone and said, "The God squad it is then." I asked what he meant by that remark? He explained that there were quite a few born-again Christians in the Fresno office, and that they had been dubbed "The God Squad." He told me I should plan on reporting around the first of the year. I was to contact his secretary to work out the details. Steve wasn't big on ceremony. After the phone call I leaned back in my chair and shook my head. What had I done? I had given up the excitement of San Francisco to manage a bunch of born-again Christians. This was going to be interesting. I may have made the biggest mistake of my career. Oh well, no looking back now. At least it should be better for the family.

We kept Terri and Tom at school in Sacramento until the summer. I commuted back and forth on weekends whenever possible. With my weeknights generally free, I continued my investigation of Christianity. What better place than an area referred to as California's Bible Belt. My goal was to complete the investigation by the time the family moved to Fresno, which Denise and I hoped would only be six months.

After my research and interviews in Sacramento, I was convinced that the Bible was one heck of a book. It was truly unique and one-of-a-kind. I believed that I had sufficient evidence to convict the Bible, beyond a reasonable doubt, of being accurate and trustworthy. In my opinion the Bible was reliable and had some supernatural influence. The odds were just too great. The case for the Bible appeared solid and airtight.

It was now time to find out more about Jesus, and the far out claim that he was God in the flesh and the savior. It was time to study the Bible, especially the New Testament. I had not told Denise that I had been convinced of the Bible's authenticity and reliability. I decided I should probably read it first. She did know that I was impressed with what I had learned thus far.

CHAPTER 15

DID JESUS ACTUALLY EXIST?

—⟋⟍⟋—

Almost everyone agrees that a man named Jesus lived here on earth. I found it rather compelling that leaders of non-Christian religions, historians, world leaders, and agnostics all believe that Jesus actually lived. After some research, I discovered the evidence supporting the existence of the man called Jesus was overwhelming. Nonetheless, there are still some skeptics who ask, "How do you know Jesus really lived, and was not a myth like other gods?"

At this stage in my investigation I considered the Bible reliable and trustworthy. The New Testament claims that Jesus lived in Israel in early A.D. and died a horrible death. In fact, Jesus is the main character in the Gospels. Biblical writings provide very specific details about Jesus' life including dates, times, places, people, events, and even quotations from him. The Gospels name his parents, relatives, friends, followers, and enemies as well as place of birth, death, and burial. All of this very detailed information could easily have been refuted if it were not true. There are no documents from that time claiming Jesus was a myth and didn't actually live. In fact, just the opposite is true. There were many who mentioned Jesus Christ in their writings. First and second century Church leaders such as Clement of Rome, Bishop Polycarp of Smyrna, Bishop Ignatuis of Antioch, and Clement of Alexandria all wrote about Jesus.

Further investigation revealed that a number of non-religious writers confirmed the existence of Jesus. Some examples include:

In A.D. 112, Roman historian Corneluis Tactus wrote that Nero, "… punished with the most exquisite tortures the persons commonly called Christians, who were hated … Christus, the founder of the name was put to death by Pontius Pilate …"

Second century satirist Lucian of Samosata alluded to Christ as, "… the man who was crucified in Palestine because he introduced this new cult into the world …"

In A.D. 112, Pliny the Younger, a governor in Asia Minor wrote that genuine Christians couldn't be induced to curse Christ. He wrote, "… they sang in alternate verse a hymn to Christ as to a god …"

Samaritan historian Thallus wrote about Jesus in A.D. 52. He explained the total darkness that took place when Jesus died on the cross as simply an eclipse of the sun, and thus not a supernatural event.

Lastly in A.D. 66, the renowned Jewish historian and Pharisee Flavius Josephus wrote, "Now there was about this time Jesus, a wise man. For he was one who wrought surprising feats and was a teacher of such people as accept the truth gladly. He won over many Jews and many of us had condemned him to be crucified, those who had in the first place come to love him did not give up their affection for him. And the tribe of Christians, so called after him has still to this day not disappeared."

There certainly seemed to be overwhelming evidence that Jesus lived in Israel during the first century. However, the big question remains, what is his true identity? Was he the Son of God or just a man who made outrageous claims?

CHAPTER 16

WHO EXACTLY IS THIS MAN NAMED JESUS?

—⁓⁓—

My investigation was approaching the most critical stage. Who was Jesus Christ? Was he a radical Jewish Rabbi, a cult leader, or the Son of God and Messiah? The answer to this puzzle was the key to Christianity, which is based on the belief that Jesus was the Son of God and Savior. If Jesus was simply a great religious leader, then Christianity was founded on a lie and thus, based upon false teachings.

This phase proved to be the most difficult part of the investigation. I wondered how I would go about finding evidence to prove or disprove such a claim. I read a number of books and parts of the Bible, but still didn't reach a conclusion. Jesus as God was a very difficult concept with obvious supernatural implications. I decided to try to find an expert on the subject. Luckily, there were a number of experts from some of the larger churches in Fresno as well as a Christian University, Fresno Pacific. The following simulated interview represents material from some of the books I read, and discussions with a number of theologians and ministers. For ease of reading, I will present my findings using the same format as in previous chapters.

The professor's administrative assistant led me into his office and made the introductions. The professor was a big man with a soft voice. He looked and shook hands like a football linebacker. He was dressed in stereotypical professor clothes consisting of slacks, white shirt and a sweater. He welcomed me with a big smile.

He spoke first, "I've been looking forward to this meeting ever since you called. I told my wife I was going to meet with a real undercover agent. She wanted to join us for the interview, but I explained that wasn't the purpose of our meeting. I've been instructed to invite you over to the house for dinner. I'll bet you have some great stories.

"That's fine with me. Tell your wife I accept the dinner invitation. With my family still in Sacramento, I could use a good home-cooked meal. I'm a little tired of fast food and Denny's specials."

He nodded, "I know what you mean. Those were my staples when I attended seminary. Nancy, my wife, will be thrilled. Do you like Italian food?"

I quickly responded, "I love it and could eat pasta every night."

"Great! How about tomorrow evening around six? I'll give you directions to the house before you leave."

"That's a date. Let's say we get started. I have a feeling this will take a while. I really appreciate you giving your valuable time to meet. I'm sure you have papers to correct or tests to grade."

He replied, "It's not a problem. In fact, I'm intrigued with your approach and investigation. This could be the beginning of a great testimony."

I shook my head, "Not so fast. I'm a long way from accepting your Christian beliefs. While I'm convinced Jesus actually lived, there is still the question of his true identity. I came here hoping that you could provide some answers based on more than just faith."

"I believe I can help on the question of who Jesus Christ really is. It is challenging to use deductive reasoning and logic to prove something supernatural. I accept the challenge."

I paused for a moment. "It appears to me that if, and that's a big if, you can show that Jesus was God and the Messiah, then the foundation of Christianity is on solid ground."

He quickly commented, "Some of us call that foundation the *Cornerstone.*"

I continued, "If you can't demonstrate that Jesus is God and the Messiah then Christianity was built on shaky grounds. Would you agree?

He answered in the affirmative, which surprised me a bit. "Absolutely. Either Jesus is or is not the Son of God. Therefore, either Christianity is or is not based on truth. There is no middle ground."

I thought about that for a moment, and agreed with his premise. He continued, "I commend you on what you've accomplished so far in your investigation. I can also appreciate the difficulty of reaching an opinion about Jesus. Many people tend to avoid reaching any type of decision about him. I think the first question to ask is, who did Jesus say he was? Did he actually claim to be God? In reviewing the Gospels of the New Testament what did you find?"

"It seemed to me that there were mixed messages in the Gospels. On the one hand he seemed to claim that he was God but on the other, he called himself the Son of Man. Can you help me out on this?"

"My pleasure! First let's clarify the use of the term, *Son of Man*. It appears over eighty times in the Gospels, and refers to a prophecy about the coming of the Messiah in the book of Daniel. It says in the book of Daniel, '… One like a Son of Man was coming …' The title, *Son of Man* refers to both the humanity and deity of Jesus."

I was amazed. "It's fascinating how you students of religion take what appears to be a difficult situation and explain it with such logical answers. Your response makes sense in the context of the entire Bible."

He smiled, "Don't be too impressed. I've been researching and studying this subject for almost forty years. I should probably have a few answers. I'm sure you are equally versed when it comes to law enforcement, particularly the drug aspect."

"Thanks. Let's continue with who Jesus said he was."

"Okay. Let's go back to the Bible. I'm convinced, as were his Jewish opponents that Jesus claimed unequivocally to be God and the promised Messiah. Let me give you a few examples. I can provide you with the exact Bible citations for your own research, if you would like."

"I would appreciate that, if it's not too much trouble."

"Not at all. In anticipation of our meeting, I printed some of them on this note pad." He continued. "Before we go on, I'm a bit curious. At this stage of your investigation, where are you leaning as to the identity of Jesus?"

Without hesitation I answered, "A very good, moral, and charismatic Jewish leader who, with his followers, started a new and somewhat radical religion."

"Thanks for your candor. Let's get back to who Jesus said he was. At his trial for blasphemy, the Jewish high priest asked Jesus pointedly, 'Are you the Christ, the Son of the blessed One?' Jesus answered that he was. That was all the Jewish leaders needed to confirm the charge of blasphemy, which was an extremely serious charge to the Jews.

Jesus had clearly claimed to be God and the Messiah. The Roman Governor, Pilate, also asked Jesus if he was the king of the Jews. Jesus responded that he was, and that his kingdom was not of this world. The Jews had no doubt as to this man's claim. When they yelled for Pilate to crucify him they said, '… He ought to die because he made himself out to be the Son of God.' When he hung on the cross they mocked him, saying that Jesus said, 'I am the Son of God.'"

He continued, "On another occasion, there was a confrontation between Jesus and the Jews. Jesus said, 'I and my Father are one.' The Jews immediately wanted to kill him by stoning for blasphemy because, 'You being a man make yourself out to be God.' Another time, Jesus commended Peter who said that Jesus was 'the Christ, the Son of the living God.' When the Samaritan woman at the well said she knew that the Messiah was coming, Jesus answered, 'I who speak to you am he.'"

He paused for a moment. "Remember the verse seen on placards at football games, John 3:16? That verse reads, 'For God so loved the world that he sent his only begotten Son that whoever believes in him shall not perish but have eternal life.' Would you like me to continue or are those enough examples for you?"

I thought for a brief time then responded, "No need to cite other examples. It's pretty clear that Jesus claimed to be the Son of God and Savior. It's also pretty clear that his followers, as well as his enemies, believed that Jesus claimed to be the Son of God. I also remember researching Old Testament prophecies predicting the Savior, and the probability that they were fulfilled in Jesus. So, where do we go from here?"

"I suppose the next step would be to determine if what Jesus claimed was actually true. Like you inferred earlier, if Jesus wasn't the Son of God and Messiah as he claimed, then Christianity is based upon false doctrine."

Curiously I asked, "How would we go about proving something like that?"

"I think deductive reasoning and logic can lead us to a legitimate conclusion on this issue. Would you agree that Jesus either is or is not the Son of God and there are no other options from which to choose?"

"I thought about that for a moment then responded, "Yes, I would agree. Either he is or he isn't. He can't be the Son of God and also not be the Son of God. As I discovered earlier in my investigation that would be considered an irreconcilable contradiction."

He responded, "You're absolutely right. Can't have it both ways. So the question to answer is, which is it? Let's examine further options under each possibility. What are the options related to Jesus being the Son of God and what are the options related to Jesus not being the Son of God?"

"That seems like a logical approach. Let's start with the premise that Jesus is not the Son of God."

"Fine. For ease of following, let's write down on that pad of paper where we are going and where we end up."

The professor took a pad of paper and wrote in the top center of the page, "Jesus said he was God." He then skipped a couple lines and wrote the words, "Two options." Skipping a couple more lines and on the left side of the paper he wrote, "Claims were false" and on the right side he wrote, "Claims were true." The paper looked like this:

Jesus said he was God

Two options

Claims were false   Claims were true

"Are you with me on this?"

"Yep, you haven't lost me so far, even though I didn't do too well in philosophy class."

"Like you, most people who are not Christians believe that Jesus was a good and wise man, great moral teacher, exceptional religious leader, and Jewish Rabbi. He is compared to Moses, Abraham, Mohammed, and other religious leaders. Would you agree?"

"Yes, that's what I believe. He stands as one of history's greatest religious leaders."

"He did however differ from other leaders like Buddha, Confucius, Mohammed, and Abraham. None of them ever claimed to be God. You and others say that he was a moral religious leader but not God as he claimed. In other words his claims were false."

"That sums up my belief."

He thought for a time and then said, "That's faulty logic and reasoning. If he wasn't God as he said, then he couldn't have been this great moral religious leader. He was a liar."

I asked, "How do you figure?"

"Think for a moment. If Jesus was not God, yet made claims that he was, then Jesus would have been either a liar or mentally disturbed. If he wasn't what he claimed to be, then those are the only two options available. Wouldn't you agree?"

I took a long time to answer; trying to come up with any other possible option. I couldn't even think of one, so I answered, "It appears that those are the only alternatives."

He took the pad and underneath *Claims were false*, he wrote on the left side, "He knew his claim was false. Thus he was a liar, fool, and evil." On the right side underneath *Claims were false* he wrote, "He didn't know his claim was false. Thus he was deluded and severely mentally ill." He then asked, "Which option do you select?"

The paper now looked like this:

Jesus said he was God

Two options

Claims were false   Claims were true

| He knew his claim was false. Thus he was a liar, fool, and evil. | He didn't know his claim was false. Thus he was deluded and severely mentally ill. |

"I never looked at it this way before. You certainly have my attention. My initial reaction is that I don't think Jesus was either a liar or insane. Isn't there another option under the heading, "Claims were false?"

"Take some time and try to come up with one."

"Weren't there some fairly sane kings who claimed deity status and really thought they were?"

"Unlike those few kings, Jesus didn't say he was like a god, or one of a number of lesser gods, or came from a god. Jesus said he was God, the one and only giver of life. So, back to my question, was Jesus a liar or insane?"

"I guess the only way to answer that is to examine his life for indications of either deceit or mental illness. I get your point. If he was a liar or deluded then he couldn't have been a good moral religious leader."

"You're right on track. Let's look at the life of Jesus to determine the feasibility of him being an evil liar and hypocrite."

I was a little taken back by all of this and responded, "You take the lead if you don't mind."

"Not at all. Saying that Jesus was evil, a liar, and hypocrite would provoke most of his greatest critics to respond, 'No way!' However, if he claimed to be God and the Savior, yet knew that he wasn't, he was a deliberate liar. He would have been a first class con man who deceived men, women, and children into thinking he was God. Those who followed him did so at significant sacrifice and risk. He would have known he was subjecting his family and closest friends to hardship and harm for a lie."

The professor continued, "He would have been the ultimate hypocrite. He repeatedly and aggressively accused others of being hypocrites because of their artificial motives. He would have been a fool since he didn't use his celebrity for power or gain. In fact, he was foolish enough to die a terrible death for the lie he created. He had numerous opportunities to recant the claim or say he was misinterpreted.

He continued, "Jesus would have been a phony for healing and forgiving people in God's name. He would have been a demon since he convinced people to trust him with their eternal salvation. He would have been a selfish imposter who lied to everyone including his mother, his brothers and sisters, and closest friends."

He stared at me and said, "Do you believe that Jesus could have been a liar, con man, hypocrite, fool, phony, demon, and selfish imposter? Do you believe that Jesus was an evil man?"

"No. I've not read anything that points to any evidence that Jesus had even one of those traits. In fact just the opposite seems to be true."

"You're right. In his three years of public ministry, Jesus was the role model for a man of character. He was good, moral, honest, caring, loving, compassionate, unselfish, and humble. Everything he did consistently demonstrated those traits. After three years, the only thing his enemies could charge him with was blasphemy for claiming he was God and the Messiah. Even his most ardent detractors credit him with being a man of good moral character. Jesus Christ was not a liar or evil man. Can we agree that if his claim to be God was false it wasn't because he was a liar?"

"Definitely. I'm convinced that Jesus was not a liar, evil, foolish, or had any of those other traits you mentioned."

"Fine. Since we are in agreement, let's move on. Let's examine the other option under the heading, His claim to be God was false. That option is that Jesus wasn't God, but actually thought he was. This means he would have had a severe mental illness. Most people who believe they are god belong in a mental institution. Jesus would have spent three years in a public ministry living in a fantasy world. He would have been a schizophrenic escaping from reality. He would have been deluded and no one noticed. Even most of his ardent critics and antagonists would respond to those allegations by claiming, 'No way!'"

He continued, "According to mental health experts and psychiatrists, mentally disturbed persons often exhibit inappropriate depression and emotions, vehement angry outbursts, and are plagued with anxiety. They are often out of touch with reality and paranoid. At times, they can't carry on a logical conversation. They tend to reach faulty conclusions and are often irrational. Does that sound like Jesus to you? Does any of your research support this contention?"

"Actually, it seems that Jesus was just the opposite. He seemed to be the model for sound mental health."

"You are right! Jesus didn't exhibit any traits of a mentally ill person. His emotions, like weeping over the death of a friend, were normal. His anger against the moneychangers in the Temple was a healthy reaction to evil. His anxiety and stress in the garden, knowing of his impending death, was natural. He knew throughout his ministry that he was in danger, but never acted paranoid. He was always in touch with reality, as exhibited by his words and actions. His thinking was rational and his speech was clear, powerful, and eloquent. He was compassionate, humble, stable, caring, accepting, and so on, despite three very demanding years of ministry. He interacted with and was loved by people from all walks of life. Jesus spoke some of the most profound words ever recorded. He actually liberated people from mental bondage. Could Jesus have been insane, mentally ill, disturbed, paranoid, schizophrenic, or deluded? There can only be one answer and that's, No! Like you said, he was the model of good sound mental health."

I asked, "I follow your line of thinking and logic, but where do we go from here?"

"If we can't show that Jesus' claims to be God are false, then the only other option is that his claims to be God and the Messiah are true. You have reached the end of your investigation. You now have sufficient evidence to convict Christianity beyond a reasonable doubt of being based on the truth. As for how you respond personally, that's up to you. You still have two options. You can accept Jesus or you can reject him."

"Wow! This is overwhelming. I need some time to digest all this information. I need to think through all of this by myself. There's got to be another answer. This was too straightforward and logical."

"I know this is a lot to absorb. Take your time. I'll be glad to help. I must warn you that I will be praying that you come to terms with your investigation, and accept Jesus as your Lord and Savior."

"Thank you. I know you are sincere. I'm kind of stunned and on information overload. I think I'll head back to my motel and watch some mindless sitcom."

"We still on for dinner?"

"Yes. I would like that."

Before I left he gave me a map to his house. He also gave me the pad he had been writing on, but added some words, so it now looked like this:

Jesus said he was God

Two options

Claims were false   Claims were true

He knew his claim was false. Thus he was a liar, fool, and evil.	He didn't know his claim was false. Thus he was deluded and severely mentally ill.	**Accept Him**	**Reject Him**

I couldn't get that discussion out of my mind that maybe, what Jesus claimed was true. Wow, what were the ramifications of that?

CHAPTER 17

ACCEPT HIM OR REJECT HIM

—⁓—

I left that evening with the words, "Accept him or reject him!" repeating over and over again in my mind. It was as if I couldn't get that thought out of my head. No doubt I had to do something or it was going to drive me crazy. I had a hard time sleeping for the next few nights as my whole investigation unfolded time and time again. The results were not what I had expected and even worse, had the potential of really complicating my life. My investigation was over and the case was closed. I needed to put it behind me and move on.

Fortunately for me, the next few weeks at work were extremely busy and hectic. There was a lot going on which occupied all my time and thoughts. Eventually, my investigation took a backseat and I thought very little about Christianity. Occasionally members of the so-called "God Squad" invited me to church, but I always had a convenient excuse. I didn't mind discussing religion with them, but even those conversations in the squad room soon ceased. It turned out that one of the agents complained to the Chief about religion being discussed at the office. I was admonished to quit engaging in religious conversations at work.

My lack of concern about Christianity lasted only until Denise struck again. When the family finally moved to Fresno, we started attending Woodward Park Baptist Church in North Fresno where we lived. The membership had quite a few leaders from the California Southern Baptist Association, since Fresno was the state headquarters. There were also some very mature Christians who attended, like Ernie Wilder, who became a good friend. It was hard to be a spectator in this small and very friendly church. Even though I was not a Christian, the whole family was active at Woodward Park. The interim pastor, Ron Chandler, started me off mowing the lawn and pulling weeds. He joked that in a Baptist Church, former Catholics needed to start at the bottom and earn their way up.

We regularly attended Sunday school where the instruction and open discussions were informative. I learned a great deal about the Bible and Christianity. I also did more than my share of challenging what was presented. The other members of the class were very patient and accepting of my "Devil's Advocate" approach to Bible study. One Sunday as I edged forward in my chair about to challenge a statement, Denise put a pencil in and across my mouth to shut me up. Needless to say everyone, including me, laughed. These were great people who took my skeptical nature in stride. Ernie was extremely patient with me, especially when I would call him late at night to question something I had read. I enjoyed learning more about the Bible and Christianity.

One day when Denise and I were alone sitting out on our patio, she asked about my investigation. I should have known better then to have that conversation with my wife. She wanted to know specific details and how I came to the final results. I told her the entire story, ending with the professor's statement about it being my choice to accept or reject Jesus. I told Denise that I chose to do neither. She looked at me and matter-of-factly said, "Given what you know, if you don't accept Jesus and his teachings, then you are choosing to reject him. I argued with her over that position, but I knew down deep she was right. This certainly isn't an area one can choose to be neutral.

That conversation led to my considering all of the reasons why I couldn't become a Christian. The trouble was that no matter what excuses I came up with, the church leaders and my Christian friends had logical answers. I originally felt that I had some legitimate reasons why I shouldn't become a Christian. Some examples of my excuses and a synopsis of the responses I received are written below. Part Three of this book has a more detailed response to some of the more challenging questions.

EXCUSE: I really like my life and don't want to change. I'll have to give up some things that I don't care to give up.

RESPONSE: Ron Climer, a Christian counselor and friend told me, "Being a Christian gives you total freedom. You don't have to give up a thing. You can do anything you want to. The only difference is that eventually God changes your want to's."

EXCUSE: I can't accept all the Christian doctrine. There are some things I have a hard time believing.

RESPONSE: You don't have to accept everything. Even the various denominations have differences, but they are still Christian Churches. They differ on such things as baptism, the Lord's Supper, sin, hell, and several other doctrines. However, they all agree on the foundation of Christianity, Jesus and the Bible. The key is to accept Jesus as your Lord and Savior, acknowledging his sacrifice on the cross for your sins. His death and resurrection are what enables a sinner like you to spend eternity with God. The beauty of Christianity is that it is your own personal relationship with God and not someone else's.

EXCUSE: I am a pretty good person. I follow most of the Ten Commandments. I know that I am better then many who call themselves Christians and go to church. I chose an occupation that serves and protects people. Why isn't that good enough?

RESPONSE: God is perfect and heaven is a place of perfection. Because we are all sinners and imperfect, we don't qualify for admission. If we sinners did gain admission then it would be blemished and no longer a place of perfection. It took the perfect sinless Jesus, being sacrificed on a cross to remove our transgressions, so that through him we could be made perfect and eligible for eternity with God.

EXCUSE: I don't want to give up control of my life.

RESPONSE: So don't. However, as you mature as a Christian you will learn that God is a great one to have in the driver's seat. That doesn't mean you become a puppet. You have and must exercise the gift of free will. You will probably find yourself depending more on guidance from the Almighty. However, you'll probably experience the see-saw effect like most Christians. We give up a degree of control and then take it back. It's a constant process, but you and God can work that out.

EXCUSE: I have a hard time with all those hypocrites who go to church and claim to be Christians.

RESPONSE: The key word is that they claim to be Christians. Just because someone goes to church or says he or she is a Christian doesn't make that person a believer. After all Tom, you go to church and aren't a Christian. I bet a number of people assume you are. Unfortunately, Christians can also be hypocrites. You should try not to let others negatively affect how you make your life decisions or what you believe. If you expect believers to be perfect then you will be sorely disappointed. Let's make one thing clear, Christians are human and sinners. Hopefully they are trying to improve their lives.

There isn't a Christian living who isn't a work in progress. As a person matures in their faith, then so too should their behavior. However, maturity doesn't simply mean knowledge or talking the talk. Maturity actually means walking the walk. Remember that churches are not showcases for saints, but rather hospitals for sinners. I admit there are some hypocrites out there that do a lot of damage to the Christian faith. Jesus appeared to be harder on hypocrites than any other sinner. He called them vipers, sons of hell, blind guides, fools, full of hypocrisy and lawlessness, and serpents. He knew the destruction they caused. One day they will have to answer for their actions.

EXCUSE: I don't see how becoming a Christian will enhance my life.

RESPONSE: First and foremost, becoming a believer assures your eternal salvation. The Bible and Jesus make that abundantly clear. That takes the guesswork and stress out of wondering what happens to you when you die. It's kind of like an insurance policy, although it's not for sale, but is freely given to you through the sacrifice of Jesus. Having the right insurance should bring a certain peace of mind. Secondly, you will find being a Christian and growing in your faith brings about a more peaceful and contented life. It's a gradual but real process, you almost have to experience to understand. Lastly, you probably will become more concerned about others, and tend to interact with people in a new way. The key to enhancing your life is to grow in your relationship with Jesus, and not remain an immature "baby" Christian. Unfortunately there are Christians who are satisfied with little or no growth. Generally their lives reflect that immaturity.

EXCUSE: I don't understand all the mysteries surrounding God. I have many questions about why certain things are the way they are. If I were God, I would have done things differently.

RESPONSE: Don't feel alone. I think if we are honest, most of us have felt the same way. I've often said that I have a lot of questions to ask when I finally get a chance to meet God. He's probably smiling knowing that once we get there all our human questions will have been answered. It's difficult to deal with supernatural concepts. As far as doing things differently than God, that may be. However, if we knew all that he knows, we might do the exact same thing. How many times have we questioned certain decisions only to realize we would have made the same decision if we had all the available information? The mysteries of God and uncovering new truths are part of the excitement of being a Christian.

EXCUSE: There is a great deal about the theory of evolution that makes sense. I tend to believe much of the scientific evidence. Isn't this in direct conflict with Christianity?

RESPONSE: Remember that evolution is a theory. However, parts of evolution are not necessarily in conflict with Christian beliefs. You can be a Christian and believe portions of the theory of evolution. There are some believers who reject any aspect of evolution. They believe that God literally made everything in six, twenty-four hour days and the earth is less than 10,000 years old. There are other Christians who believe the seven days were long segments of time and the earth is millions of years old. They also believe that God could have used evolution in his creation process. Both groups are still Christians. They both believe God is the creator and reject the theory that all creation came about by chance, and there is no God.

EXCUSE: How can a loving God allow so much pain and suffering to exist?

RESPONSE: In the beginning God made everything good. There was no evil or pain. Thus God is the author of all that is good. God also gave his beings the gift of free will. He didn't make robots or puppets. He gave us the ability to choose. We could choose to love him or not love him. God's desire was for us to love freely; otherwise it wouldn't truly be love. One of God's celestial creations, referred to as Satan, used his free will and chose to rebel against God. He committed the first act of evil. Because Heaven is a place of perfection, Satan through his sin could no longer remain with God. He was cast out of heaven to earth where he reigns. Satan is the author of all evil. All pain and sin can be traced directly back to him. We have a free will and sin is a choice. Do you remember the story of the Garden of Eden and Satan's influence? The Bible tells us that good will eventually defeat evil.

EXCUSE: I'm not ready right now. Maybe I'll become a believer later.

RESPONSE: Later may be too late!

EXCUSE: I'm concern that I might think I've accepted Jesus only to find out later that I was wrong. I've seen people at events go forward to accept Jesus only to discover that it was an emotional decision and not genuine. I don't want to make a commitment and not follow through. I want to avoid being a Christian today and non-Christian tomorrow.

RESPONSE: I respect your integrity. When the time is right and you pray the sinner's prayer to accept Jesus as your Lord, you will know whether it was genuine. Just be open and talk with God about it. You'll get your answer, and will know beyond a doubt that you have become a believer.

I was running out of excuses. I found myself in a very tough situation. I usually had my stuff together and was very self-assured. This Christian thing was confusing me and taxing my brain. I remember wishing that I could accept it on faith like so many, including my wife. She seemed so at peace.

CHAPTER 18

ACCEPT HIM

—⟋⟍—

After a lot of soul searching, I decided that there was no longer any excuse not to accept Jesus. The question was how to proceed and have it be legitimate. I had heard about what some people called the sinner's prayer. It goes something like this, "Jesus, I'm a sinner and I ask your forgiveness. I accept that you died on the cross for my sins and rose again for my salvation. I surrender my life to you and receive you as my Lord and Savior."

How and when do I pray this prayer? I don't want to tell Denise that I became a believer and have it not be real. She would certainly know if it was real or not. This all seemed quite confusing. Was I just making it more difficult then it was? The answer came when members of the "God Squad" invited Denise and me to a Police Couples Conference at Hume Lake Christian Camp near Kings National Park.

Hume Lake was about an hour east of Fresno. We arrived on a Friday afternoon, and checked into our five bedroom cabin with four other couples. We could have stayed in the dorms but our group, who attended at least annually, preferred the cabin. What a gorgeous setting, high in the Sierra Mountains with a pristine lake surrounded by tall pines! It felt like a little touch of heaven. We went to the group dinner and met the leaders and the other couples who sat at our dinner table. There must have been a hundred cops and their spouses. That evening we had the first devotional. The presentation was down to earth and perfect for police couples. The main speaker was Assistant Chief Bob Vernon from the Los Angles Police Department.

Saturday was just as inspiring and appropriate. The food was great and the messages held my interest. We had an afternoon recreational break. Denise and I went canoeing on the lake. It was so peaceful and relaxing. That evening after dinner we had our last presentation. Assistant Chief Vernon asked the group to leave the auditorium and find a solitary spot to reflect on their relationship with God. He suggested we pray for a closer more personal relationship. He also encouraged those who were not believers to pray about accepting Jesus as their Savior. We all left and were asked to return within a half hour for the late evening snacks.

I hiked about five minutes up the mountain and found a dead tree trunk lying on the ground in a secluded place. It was a warm spring night, illuminated by the full moon, and surrounded by millions of bright stars. I sat on the trunk and struck up a conversation with God. It went something like this: Okay, I quit. I can't think of any good reason why I shouldn't surrender right here and now. I'm convinced that your son, Jesus Christ is the Savior. I'd love to have my many sins forgiven. I want to follow him and be saved. I only have one reservation and want to ask a favor. Please make sure if I do this that it's a take. Please make sure that I'm a true believer who won't reject you at a later time. Do we have a deal? Sorry, I probably shouldn't be making deals with you. I should just step out in faith. As you know that's real hard for me. I am a skeptic by nature. So here we go. God, I want to be born again, only this time spiritually. Are you ready? I guess I'm as ready as I will ever be. If I can't do it here in this beautiful and spiritual setting, I'll probably never be able to do it.

Ready, here goes, "Dear Lord, I'm a sinner and truly ask forgiveness. I'm so sorry for all the wrong things that I've done in my life. Please forgive me. I surrender my life to you, and accept the sacrifice of your death on the cross for my sins and salvation. Thank you for that free gift. I humbly accept you as my Lord and Savior. Help me live my life worthy of you."

As I prayed, I became uncommonly emotional and tears actually trickled down my cheek. These were tears of joy. I felt so at peace. It was as if a load had been lifted from me, that I hadn't known existed. About a half hour passed when I started back down the mountain to the auditorium. As I walked I continued to pray, "You know God, it would be great to get some kind of a sign to make sure this is the real deal. I'm almost 100% sure, but I certainly would feel more comfortable telling Denise if you let me know that you accepted my prayer of surrender to you."

About that time, for some reason, I turned around and looked up at the moon which was behind me. There was a small black cloud partially covering it. My immediate thought was, "Is this any kind of a sign? That would really be cool!" I continued down the mountain. Just a few minutes before I got to the camp I stopped and looked back at the moon. The dark cloud was gone and the moon was bright. I immediately yelled out loud, "I'll take it!"

I started jogging back to the auditorium and noticed that everyone was back inside. Everyone, that is, but one very special person. In a small clearing near the entrance door, I saw Denise with nobody around. I ran up to her and grabbed her in a tight hug. Then as my eyes watered, I kissed her cheek and said, "Thank you babe, I just accepted Jesus as my Lord and Savior." We held each other for a long time and cried tears of happiness. I can't imagine how Denise must have felt. Needless to say we missed our late evening snack, but still felt totally filled. Yes, life is good!

PART TWO

THE EVIDENCE

—⁓—

CHAPTER 19

INTRODUCTION

—〜〜—

Part Two contains the majority of the material and evidence that I collected during my investigation. The purpose of this section is twofold. The first is to provide skeptics and/or non-believers with more detailed information to study and research as they consider their spiritual life. The second is to increase the knowledge and confidence level of Christians in defending their faith. Part Two is designed to be used for either self-study or in small groups. At the conclusion of this section, the reader should be able to present compelling evidence showing beyond a reasonable doubt that the Bible is accurate and trustworthy, and that Jesus is God and the Messiah.

Part Two begins with some Bible background such as; who determined which books belonged in the Bible, what is the difference between the Jewish and Christian Old Testament, what is the Apocrypha, what are the Gnostic Gospels, and why are the Dead Sea Scrolls so important? The study continues by providing evidence establishing that the Bible is unique, reliable, and accurate. Part Two then addresses Biblical criticism by covering topics such as; could all those animals have fit in the Ark, was it possible for Jonah to have lived in the belly of a whale for three days, and what about all the errors and contradictions in the Bible? This section concludes by presenting evidence showing that Jesus Christ is God and the Messiah.

HOW TO STUDY

There is a substantial amount of detailed material in Part Two. If you're like me and possess average (at best) mental capability, I suggest that you read one chapter, reflect on what you have read, and then go over the review questions at the end of the chapter. Repeat this process chapter by chapter. Don't try to cover too much at one time. I find retention can be a problem. Should you still have questions after finishing Part Two, I recommend that you take time to research the answer. If you possess superior intellect or are a gifted individual then please disregard my suggestions.

If you remain stuck on a particular point, you are welcome to send me your question(s) and I will try to provide an answer. I can be reached at P O Box 3364, Evergreen, Colorado 80437

In case you would like to explore a particular topic in more detail, I have provided numbers (2/13) preceding or following a section or paragraph indicating the specific reference book and page number(s) in which the material can be found. The reference section at the back of the book lists the reference material corresponding to the first number found in the parentheses. Generally the reference book has greater detail and covers the subject more fully.

You may disagree with some of the statements or aspects of this book. Other parts may not be very convincing. That's fine. However, try not to let that distract from considering the preponderance of evidence. Like a juror during a trial, you don't have to accept all the evidence. However, in the end, a juror must decide if overall there is sufficient direct and/or circumstantial evidence to reach a conclusion beyond a reasonable doubt.

As I stated in the acknowledgment, this book only touches the surface of many important topics. It is nothing more than an executive summary or synopsis of the hard work and research of many others. Hopefully this book will motivate you to increase your knowledge of Christian apologetics. If so, I strongly encourage you to review the list of reference material, and read some if not all of those outstanding books.

ICE BREAKER

If you chose to use Part Two for a small group, the leader may want to ask these questions to generate discussion and interaction:

- What is your first memory of the Bible?
- Recite or paraphrase one of your favorite Bible verses? Why is it meaningful to you?

- Can you briefly describe a time, other than Bible study or daily devotion, that you turned to the Bible for a specific reason?
- What version of the Bible do you read and why?
- Give a couple word description of the Bible.

THOUGHT TO CONSIDER

As with most Americans, we have a great deal of reverence for the American Flag, the National Anthem, and the Statue of Liberty. Rightfully so! We are proud to be Americans and honor those symbols representing our great country. Do you feel the same way about being a Christian? Are you proud to be called a follower of Jesus Christ? Do you honor and cherish the symbols of your faith?

Take a few moments to reflect on the Bible. Why doesn't there seem to be the same degree of reverence for the Holy Bible as there is for the Constitution? Shouldn't we be humbled and awed every time we read Scripture, and realize the words were inspired by God? The Bible is truly one-of-a-kind!

INTERESTING FACTS ABOUT THE BIBLE
(12 & 15)

- It is the best selling book of all time.
- The Old Testament (OT) contains 39 books, 929 chapters, 23,214 verses, and 622,771 words.

- The New Testament (NT) contains 27 books, 260 chapters, 7,959 verses, and 184,590 words.
- The shortest chapter is Psalms 117 and the longest is Psalms 119.
- Shortest verse in the OT is 1 Chronicles 1:25 ("Eber, Peleg, Reu").
- Shortest verse in the NT is John 11:35 ("Jesus wept").
- Noah was the first person mentioned as being intoxicated from wine.
- Song of Solomon and Esther are the only two books that don't mention God.
- There are over 600 commandments in the Law of Moses.
- Psalms 14 and Psalms 53 are virtually identical.
- King Solomon had the equivalent of 1000 wives.
- In 1456 the Gutenberg press produced the first printed Bible.
- The oldest known fragment of Biblical text dates from 587 B.C.
- Goliath was a little over nine feet tall.
- Men take note; dogs are mentioned a couple dozen times, while cats are not mentioned at all.
- There is only one street named in the NT that being "Straight Street." in Damascus (Acts 9:11). The street still exists.
- Zachariah is the most common name in the Bible (over 30).

- The most frequent named used for Jesus is "Son of Man" (over 80 times).
- Judas Iscariot was the only apostle who did not come from the region of Galilee.

CHAPTER 20

BIBLE BACKGROUND

—ʍ—

In what language was the Bible written? (11)

Actually, the Bible was written in three languages. The New Testament was written in the first century universal language, Greek. The majority of the Old Testament was written in Hebrew except for ten chapters, which were written in Aramaic. These were; Jeremiah 10:11, Daniel 2:4 to 7:28, Ezra 4:8 to 6:18, Ezra 7:12-26, and two words in Genesis 31:47.

Aramaic is a Jewish dialect from Syria dating as far back as the fourteenth century B.C. It eventually became the common language of the Jews. Jesus spoke Galilean Aramaic.

What method(s) was commonly used to record the text of the Bible? (2/25-27 & 18/120)

Writing material included:

- *Papyrus* was the most common ancient writing material until about the third century

141

A.D. It came from the papyrus plant. Strips from the center of the plant were laid out in sheets. This reed grew along the Nile River in Egypt and also in Syria. The Papyrus sheets survived best in a dry climate but were perishable over time. According to custom, the primary shipping point for papyrus in Phoenicia was the city of Byblos, believed to be named by the Greeks after their word for *books* (Biblos). This was the origin of our term, *Bible*. The English word *paper* comes from the word papyrus.

- *Parchment* was specially prepared animal skins used as writing material. Jewish leaders preferred that Scripture be written on animal skins as it was more substantial and would last longer. Vellum, the skin from young animals, was a finer grade of parchment.

- *Pen* was a pointed reed usually 6 to 12 inches long. The reed was cut with a knife to form a flexible point. Scribes often carried these knives with them to keep the pen points usable for writing. That's how we got the word, *pen knife*. The reed pen was used from the beginning of writing on papyrus to about the third century B.C. The quill pen eventually replaced the reed.

- *Ink* was usually a compound of soot or charcoal and gum mixed in water.

Ancient books:

- *Scrolls* consisted of sheets of papyrus glued together and wound around a rod. The writing was usually on one side of the papyrus. Scrolls averaged from 20 to 35 feet long, but some were much longer.
- *Codex* consisted of papyrus sheets written on both sides assembled in binders. This book form was primarily developed because of the dependence on writing by the early Christian movement.
- *Miscellaneous Information*: Greek manuscripts did not have breaks between words. Hebrew was written right to left and without vowels. The first use of chapters was in 586 B.C., when part of the Old Testament was divided into the Pentateuch or first five books. Verses were divided sporadically until the first standard division around A.D. 900.

Who determined which books would make up the official Bible?

Canon is the term used to describe the officially accepted books of Scripture. Canon comes from the root word, *reed* which was used as a standard measuring rod. Thus canon means the standard.

How was the Old Testament canon established?
(2/30-33, 11, 18/112-115 & 19/66-70)_

Scholars aren't entirely positive of all the factors used to determine which books to include in the Old

Testament. They do know that Jewish leaders applied some standard tests on writings that were examined. They included:

1) Did the writings come from God? The Old Testament used words like, "... *The Lord God said ...*" thousands of times to show that God, not the writer was ultimately responsible for what was written.

2) Was it written by a person of God and/or prophet?

3) Was it accurate and reliable?

4) Was it consistent with other accepted books of the Old Testament?

Different parts of the Old Testament were accepted at different times. For instance, the first five books called the Torah or Pentateuch were accepted around the Babylonian Supremacy (625-539 B.C.). The scrolls that made up the Prophets were probably recognized as part of Jewish Scripture between 250-175 B.C. The last section often called the Writings must have been accepted sometime before Jesus since he referred to all three divisions during his ministry.

The early Jewish Scripture was not formed into books, but rather consisted of a number of scrolls. Each scroll contained one or a group of writings which we now call books of the Old Testament. Their canon included 24 writings or books formed into three subsections: 1) Law 2) Prophets 3) Writings.

The Old Testament in the Christian Bible is the same as the Jewish Bible except it includes 39 books and doesn't follow the exact same order. The additional books are actually not more books, but rather some have been divided into two parts. For instance, the Jewish Bible has one book of Samuel, Kings, Chronicles, and Ezra/Nehemiah. The Christian Bible divides Samuel, Kings, and Chronicles each into two books. It also separates Ezra/Nehemiah into two books. The Jewish Bible counts the twelve Minor Prophets as one book ("The Twelve") rather than twelve separate books, as does the Christian Bible. Jewish Scripture includes:

LAW: Genesis, Exodus, Leviticus, Numbers, and Deuteronomy

PROPHETS: Joshua, Judges, Samuel, Kings, Isaiah, Jeremiah, Ezekiel, and The Twelve

WRITINGS: Psalms, Proverbs, Job, Song of Songs, Ruth, Lamentations, Esther, Ecclesiastes, Daniel, Ezra/Nehemiah, and Chronicles

Support for the Old Testament canon includes:
- Christ himself testified to the three subsections of the Jewish Bible. Luke 24:44 quotes Jesus as saying, "… that all things which are written about me in the Law of Moses and the Prophets and the Psalms must be fulfilled." The word, Psalms was sometimes used in place of the subsection, Writings. That was because Psalms was the first and longest book of that section. Jesus quoted from the Old Testament frequently, testifying to it's validity as Scripture and references to him as

the Messiah. A few examples of his words of this issue include:

- ➤ John 10:34, "… Has it not been written in your Law …" (Reference to: The Law and Jeremiah 1:5)
- ➤ John 6:45, " It is written in the Prophets, 'And they shall be taught of God.'…" (Reference to: Isaiah 54:13)
- ➤ Luke 10:26-27, "… What is written in the Law? …" he answered and said, "You shall love the Lord … and you neighbor as yourself." (Reference to: Deuteronomy 6:5 and Leviticus 19:18)
- ➤ Luke 11:51, "… from the blood of Abel to the blood of Zechariah …" (Reference to: Genesis, the first book to Chronicles, the last book)
- ➤ Mark 12:10, "Have you not even read this Scripture: 'The stone which the builder rejected has become the chief corner stone.'" (Reference to: Psalms 118:22)
- ➤ Mark 7:6-10, "… Rightly did Isaiah prophesy of you hypocrites, as it is written … For Moses said …" (Reference to: Isaiah. 29:13 and Exodus.20:12)
- ➤ Matthew 6:29, "… even Solomon in all his glory did not clothe himself

like one of these." (Reference to: 2 Chronicles 9:22)

➤ Matthew 11:10, "This is about whom it is written, 'Behold, I send my Messenger ..., who will prepare your way before you.'" (Reference to: Malachi.3:1)

In Matthew alone, Jesus used sixty individual references from fifteen out of the twenty-four books of the Old Testament. There are similar references in the other Gospels by Mark, Luke, and John. Jesus accepted and validated the majority of Jewish Scripture.

- Early Jewish writers testified to the Old Testament canon. The Jewish historian, Josephus, toward the end of the first century wrote, "... and how firmly we have given credit to those books ... no one has been so bold as either to add anything to them or take anything from them or to make any changes in them ... to esteem those books to contain divine doctrines ... willing to die for them ..." (2/31)
- The New Testament certifies the Old Testament as being Sacred Scripture. A few examples include:

  ➤ Acts 17:2, "And according to Paul's custom ... reasoned with them from the Scriptures,"

  ➤ Acts 18:28, "for he [Apollos] power- fully refuted the Jews in public,

> demonstrating by the Scriptures that Jesus was the Christ."

➤ Romans 4:3, "For what does the Scripture say? 'And Abraham believed God, and it was reckoned to him as righteousness.'"

➤ I Corinthians 15:3, "… Christ died for our sins according to Scripture,"

➤ II Timothy 3:16, "All Scripture is inspired by God and profitable for …"

➤ II Peter 1:20, "But know this first of all, that no prophecy of Scripture is a matter of one's own interpretation."

Shortly after the fall of Jerusalem in A.D. 70, the Sanhedrin (Jewish Supreme Court) was reconstituted in Jamnia. The result of the Council of Jamnia was to officially recognize all the books of the Old Testament as Holy Scripture. The Christian Church officially accepted the Jewish Bible (Old Testament) in the fourth century A.D.

How was the New Testament canon determined?
(4/37-39, 18/130-133 & 27/152-154)

The Church fathers used a number of tests to determine which books to include in the New Testament. From A.D. 170-350 leaders studied, examined, and tested writings for inclusion in the Bible. Initially they only accepted the four Gospels, Acts, the thirteen letters of Paul, I Peter, and I John. By A.D. 200 the books of the New Testament were largely settled.

In A.D. 397 at the Council of Carthage, the 27 books were firmly fixed and have remained that way. The most disputed are said to have been Hebrews, II Peter, 2 & 3 John, Jude, James, and Revelation.

Some tests believed to have been used include:

- Was it written by an apostle or under the authority of an apostle?
- Did it accurately reflect the teachings and life of Jesus and the apostles?
- Was it written at a time that witnesses to the events were still living?
- Was it authentic? The early church leaders followed a policy that could be summed up as, "If in doubt then throw it out."
- Was it accepted by the followers of Jesus and the Church?
- Were the contents consistent with having been inspired by God and with the other accepted books of the New Testament?
- Was it historically or geographically accurate?
- Did it teach and foster Christian doctrine?

What is the Apocrypha? (11 & 12/889-892)

The Apocrypha is a Greek term that means "hidden or concealed." It is the fourteen books included in the Old Testament of the Roman Catholic Bible and reaffirmed by the Church between 1545 and 1563 at the Council of Trent. These books are rejected by Protestants and Jews. The books include:

1) <u>Wisdom of Solomon</u> was written in Greek between 150-50 B.C. by an Alexandrian Jew. The

theme is wisdom and righteousness and denunciation of iniquity and idolatry.

2) <u>Wisdom of Jesus, son of Sirach also known as Ecclesiasticus</u> was written in Hebrew between 200-175 B.C. by a scholar from Jerusalem. It is the only book of the group where the author is known. It is also the longest book. Like Proverbs, it covers a variety of practical subjects from diet to domestic relationships.

3) <u>Esther</u> was written during the second and third century B.C. by an Egyptian Jew. The author translated the book of Esther into Greek but added 107 verses. The additional verses include ten to Esther 10 and six new chapters (11-16).

4) <u>Prayer of Manasseh</u> was written during the last two centuries B.C. by a Palestinian Jew. The prayer is attributed to Manasseh, King of Judah, who was taken prisoner to Babylon where he repented of idolatry that characterized his reign.

5) <u>Song of the Three Young Men</u> was written in Hebrew by a pious Jew during the Maccabean revolt (175-135 B.C.). This was added to the book of Daniel and is a prayer of praise for deliverance from a furnace.

6) <u>Susanna</u> was written in Hebrew or Greek during the first or second century B.C. Nothing is known about the author. The book is a story of how Daniel saved the life of Susanna who was falsely accused of adultery. He showed the witnesses against her had lied.

7) <u>Bel and the Dragon</u> was written in Hebrew in the middle of the first century B.C. Nothing is

known about the author. This book tells of Daniel destroying the objects of Babylonian worship (Bel and the Dragon) and his escape from the lions den. It was added to the book of Daniel.

8) I Maccabees was written in Hebrew about 100 B.C. by a Palestinian Jew. This book relates the history between 175-135 B.C. during the Jewish resistance and Maccabean Wars, which led to an independent Jewish State. Hanukkah, which Jews celebrate at Christmas, commemorates the rededication of the Temple as a result of Maccabees' bravery. John 10:22 refers to this as, "The Feast of the Dedication."

9) II Maccabees was written in Greek about 120 B.C. by an Alexandrian Jew. It parallels I Maccabees' first seven chapters (175-160 B.C.) but stresses less history and a more mystic aspect of the revolt.

10) Tobit was written in Aramaic during the second century B.C. Nothing is known about the author. The book is a love story between Tobit's son Tobias and a virgin widow. The story involves defeating an evil spirit.

11) Judith was written in Hebrew by a Palestinian Jew after the Maccabean revolt. This is a story of how Judith delivers her people from an Assyrian commander by getting him drunk and cutting off his head.

12) Esdras was written in Aramaic toward the end of the first century A.D. by a Jew. The book parallels some of 2 Chronicles, Ezra, and Nehemiah as well as relating a series of episodes from the Old Testament.

13) Baruch could have partially been written around 600 B.C. by Jeremiah's friend and secretary, Baruch.

It includes other authors and was not completed until first century B.C. Some of the book is written in Greek and some in Hebrew. The book consists of prayers and confessions of the Jews in exile.

14) <u>Letter of Jeremiah</u> was written in Hebrew in about 300 B.C. by an unknown author. The book is an impassioned sermon about the impotence of the gods of wood, silver, and gold based on Jeremiah 11:10.

When reviewing a Catholic Bible all the books of the Apocrypha don't appear to be included. That is because some are combined with other books in the Old Testament. For instance Bel and the Dragon and the Song of the Three Young Men were included in the Book of Daniel. The Letter of Jeremiah was folded into Baruch as one book.

Why was the Apocrypha rejected as inspired Scripture? (11 & 12/889-892)

The Apocrypha is of literary and historical value, but was rejected because religious leaders concluded:

- The books have historical and geographical errors.
- The Apocrypha teaches doctrine and practices opposed to accepted Scripture.
- The books were known to Jesus and the apostles but they never quoted from them as authoritative Scripture. The Apocrypha was not part of the Old Testament used by Jesus or the early church.

- The books were known to the ancient Jewish writers but they never quoted from them as Scripture.
- The Apocrypha was distinguished from the Old Testament writings by early church fathers.
- The Apocrypha books were not included as Scripture in the original Hebrew version of the Old Testament used in the Holy Land during the time of Jesus. . The Jewish community in A.D. 90 rejected the Apocrypha as Scripture.

What are the Dead Sea scrolls? (2/57-58 & 12/1271-1274)

In 1947, a shepherd boy named Muhammad was searching for a lost goat. This was on the west side of the Dead Sea about eight miles south of Jericho. He tossed a stone into a hole in a cliff and heard the shattering of pottery. Investigating, he discovered several large jars on the floor of a cave. They contained scrolls wrapped in linen cloth. It's believed they were placed in the caves about A.D. 68. The documents were between 1850 to 2150 years old. The scrolls were written in Hebrew and Aramaic. Additional manuscripts have subsequently been found in other caves. These documents were written from 200 B.C. to A.D. 68. The scrolls contain both Biblical and non-Biblical material. They contain the complete book of Isaiah and parts or fragments of all the other books of the Old Testament except Esther. Radiocarbon tests and paleographic evidence (examination of letter-forms) confirmed the dates.

What is the Torah?

The first five books of the Old Testament written by Moses consisting of Genesis, Exodus, Leviticus, Numbers, and Deuteronomy. Torah means Law and Jesus referred to it as the Law of Moses.

What is the Pentateuch?

It is the same as the Torah or Law. *Penta* in Greek means five i.e. first five books of the Old Testament.

What are the Synoptic Gospels?

The Gospels of Matthew, Mark, and Luke because of the similarity of the events and facts reported by all three. The Synoptic Gospels presented a common view. The fourth Gospel, John is somewhat different. Synoptic comes from the Greek word *sunopsis*, which means blended view.

What are the Gnostic Gospels? (30)

In the second century, a semi-religious movement related to Christianity was established. This movement was called Gnosticism. The so-called intellectual Gnostic leaders taught that people could achieve salvation only by acquiring knowledge (gnosis). They tended to revise Christian theology to help answer certain questions and address a variety of topics. Their views on God, Jesus, sin, salvation, judgment, and resurrection were found solely in their own teachings. Most accepted an impersonal and remote God. Many believed a supernatural evil being called Demiurge created the world. Gnostics felt that the world was ruled by evil spirits, but certain select persons possessed a divine spark. Through knowledge this spark could be freed from the evil world and be with God. They believed that Jesus was a divine messenger who brought knowledge to Christians. They did not believe he was man nor did they believe in the resurrection.

They were responsible for writing books supporting their philosophy. These books have been referred to as the Gnostic gospels which were found at Nag Hammadi, Egypt in 1945. Some include; Gospel of Philip, Gospel of Mary, Gospel of Thomas, Gospel of Truth, Apocalypse of Paul, and Letter of Peter to Philip. They were written 100 to 200 years after the life of Jesus. None of these books were written by the person for whom the book was named, as they were all deceased by that time.

What about all the different versions of the Bible?

Most of the different versions or translations are based on the earliest manuscripts of the Bible. The different versions were primarily developed for style and readability. Some of the popular ones include; the *King James Version*, the *New American Standard Bible*, the *New Living Translation*, the *New International Version,* and the *Douay Bible* (Roman Catholic Bible). The *King James Version* is written in old English and considered by many as an example of classical use of the language. Although at one time it was used by most Protestant Christians, many have found it difficult to read and understand. There is the *New Living Translation* which is often paraphrased and easy to read using everyday simple language. The *New American Standard Bible* and *New International Version* try to use exact translations of the original words as much as the English language will allow.

The best way to study the Bible is to use a commentary. Good commentaries will provide an objective view of the meaning or possible meanings of the verses. It will often provide the original word used and its definition, the context within which the verse was written, and some cultural background. Commentaries can help explain passages that may be difficult to understand. I'm personally amazed how often after reviewing commentaries that my questions are answered. I have found myself saying, "Wow, those guys who wrote the Bible were smart." My wife will add, "I think they had a little help from a friend."

The easiest way to explain the different versions is that most try to stick as close as possible to the original meaning. They differ basically in style as well as ease of reading and understanding. The Greek language has many more words to relay a meaning than English. For example, Greeks have at least three words for love, whereas we only have one. That could affect the meaning if you didn't know which "love" the New Testament writers were using. According to the best selling book, "The Purpose Driven Life," the Bible was written using over eleven thousand Hebrew and Greek words for which we use only six thousand words.

REVIEW

1. What language was the New Testament written in and why?
2. What does canon mean in relationship to the Bible?
3. What is the best evidence that the Old Testament canon is inspired Scripture?
4. How does the Jewish Old Testament differ from that used by Christians?
5. Name some of the tests used to determine which books to include in the New Testament.
6. What is the Apocrypha? Why wasn't it accepted as part of the Protestant Bible?
7. Why is the discovery of the Dead Sea scrolls so important?
8. What is: The Torah? The Pentateuch? The Synoptic Gospels?
9. Explain why you use a particular version of the Bible.

CHAPTER 21

EVIDENCE SUPPORTING THE BIBLE

—⁓⁓—

THE BIBLE IS UNIQUE
(2/16-24 & 26)

Unique is defined as something that is in a class of its own. Something that is different from all others and having no equals. The Bible is undeniably unique. Even some of its most ardent critics would agree. This claim is based on a number of factors, including but not limited to:

- It was written over a 1500 year time span from approximately 1400 B.C. to A.D.100.
- The Bible was written by over 40 authors from a variety of backgrounds. Some like Peter and John were simple fishermen. Others like Moses and Daniel were political leaders. Luke was a doctor, Joshua was a military leader, and Matthew was a tax collector. Biblical authors included two kings, Solomon and David. Probably the most notable author

159

was the apostle Paul, who before he was converted, persecuted followers of Jesus.

- The Bible was written from different locations on three different continents (Asia, Africa and Europe). Parts of the book were written from a prison, desert, island, small village, and a palace.
- The Bible was written in three different languages (Hebrew, Aramaic & Greek).
- The Bible is the most read book in history. By the year 2002, the Bible had been published in 392 languages with parts published in additional languages. There have been more copies produced than any other book (billions). The Bible has been and continues to be a best seller. According to the International Bible Society approximately 168,000 Bibles are sold or given away daily in the United States alone.
- The Bible has successfully survived more criticism and persecution than any other book.
- Regardless of all the above factors, this truly unique book contains only one central theme. That is, God's relationship with and redemption of mankind.

Consider the odds of eight authors, from different backgrounds, over a 40 year time span, and from at least six different locations all writing about a very controversial subject with such harmony and agreement. That describes the New Testament.

This chapter is a brief summary, that doesn't purport to answer all the questions about the uniqueness of the Bible. You are encouraged to do your own research. For instance, research Islam's Koran, Hindu's Bhagavad-Gita, Buddhist's The Three Baskets or any other religion's "scriptures" and contrast them to the Bible. You will find that there is no comparison. In fact, compare the Bible to any book of your choosing. I believe you will find it has no equals. However, I invite you to do your own research and draw your own conclusions.

BIBLE IS RELIABILE AND TRUSTWORTHY
(4/42-117 & 7/59-83)

Many will agree that the Bible is in a class of its own, but question its reliability. Can what is written be trusted as accurate? That's a legitimate question that should be answered, particularly if the Bible is used to help formulate a person's belief system. The Bible should be validated by applying the same examination used to judge other historical books or documents. If the Bible can't pass this time-tested examination, first developed by Aristotle, then it should probably be regarded skeptically.

The study of the reliability of historic documents has been called historiography or textual criticism. It consists of three primary parts: 1) Bibliographical test 2) Internal evidence test 3) External evidence test.

BIBLIOGRAPHICAL TEST

This test examines how accurate the current text is in relationship to the original writing. In other words, is what we are reading today substantially the same as how the ancient work was originally written? Most of what we know and believe about the past was recorded in writing by historians. How accurate is what we read about the history of Rome or Greece? How similar is what we are reading by Plato, Homer, or Aristotle compared to what they actually wrote? Three major areas are considered in determining the accuracy of the current text compared to the original document:

1) How many different ancient manuscripts exist?
2) How close in time are the ancient manuscripts to the time the document was originally written?
3) How accurate is the current text translation compared to the ancient manuscripts?

New Testament manuscripts

The greater the number of ancient manuscripts and the closer in time that they are to the original writing; the more trustworthy the document. Also, the fewer differences (textual variations) between the ancient manuscripts and the current document the more reliable the current document.

The following chart provides a comparison of some respected ancient works. Compare the number of manuscripts, and the length of time between the manuscripts and the original writing. In this category, no other ancient document compares to the Bible. The nearest is the *Iliad* written by Homer, which has 643 surviving copies with the oldest only 500 years from the original writing. The Bible has over 5,000 surviving copies with the earliest written within 25 to 85 years of the original. (4/45):

Work	Written	Earliest copy	Time span	# of copies
Homer's *Iliad*	900 B.C.	400 B.C.	500 yrs	643
Caesar's *Gallic Wars*	100-44 B.C.	A.D. 900	1000 yrs	10
Herodotus on Greece	480-425 B.C.	A.D. 900	1300 yrs	8
Pliny's *History of Rome*	A.D. 61-113	A.D. 850	750 yrs	7
Aristotle's writings	384-322 B.C.	A.D.1100	1400 yrs	49
New Testament	A.D. 40-100	A.D. 125	25-85 yrs	5,000+

The last part of the bibliographical test tries to determine the accuracy of the current translation. Textual criticism experts have carefully studied the wording in the oldest manuscripts of the New Testament. They compared this wording to that of the modern New Testament translation. What they discovered was less than one half of one percent error (corruption) rate. That equates to only 400 out of 184,590 words. Compare that to over 5% for the *Iliad* and 10% for the *Mahabharata* (History of India). A 5% or 10% error rate is fairly good when considering the length of time involved. One half of one percent is incredible, especially since that most of the errors are either style or spelling and not substantial variations. (2/43)

Sir Frederic Kenyon an authority on New Testament textual criticism writes, "No fundamental doctrine of the Christian faith rests on a disputed reading ..."

"It cannot be too strongly asserted that in substance the text of the Bible is certain: Especially is this the case with the New Testament. The number of manuscripts of the New Testament, of early translations from it, and of quotations from it in the oldest writers of the Church, is so large that it is practically certain that the true reading of every doubtful passage is preserved in some one or other of these ancient authorities. *This can be said of no other book in the world.*"

"Scholars are satisfied that they possess substantially the true text of the principal Greek and Roman writers ... yet knowledge of their writings depends on a mere handful of manuscripts, whereas the manuscripts of the New Testament are counted by the hundreds, and even thousands." (4/46)

Dr.Gleason Archer of Trinity Divinity School in answer to an inquiry responded, "A careful study of the variants [different readings] of the various earliest manuscripts reveals that none of them affects a single doctrine of Scripture ..." (4/46) Critics of the Bible cannot refute these statements.

The New Testament has the added support of early church writings that quoted different verses. These writings provided very early confirmation of the words used in the original. This also confirms the reliability of what we read in today's Bible. The early church leader's writings date from A.D. 70 to 250. These leaders included Clement of Alexandria, Ignatius of Antioch, Origen, Tertullian of Carthage, and Irenaeus of Lyons. There were over 36,000 quotations from the New Testament written before the Council of Nicaea in A.D. 325. According to Bible scholar, F.F. Bruce there is 19,368 quotations from the Gospels and 14,035 from Paul's letters. The additional quotations were from the Book of Acts, the other letters, and Revelation. Harold Greenlee, an expert in ancient documents states that New Testament quotations by early church leaders, "... are so extensive that the N. T. could virtually be reconstructed from them without the use of the New Testament manuscripts." (2/50) Sir David Dalrymple was asked, if all New Testaments were destroyed was there enough written by the early church leaders to reconstruct it. After substantial investigation he responded, "... I possessed all the existing works of the Fathers of the second and third centuries, I commenced to search, and up to this time I have found the entire New Testament, except eleven verses." (2/50-52)

Old Testament manuscripts (4/48-51, 7/60-63 & 12)

The number of Old Testament manuscripts and their proximity to the original writing is similar to that of other ancient works. For instance, the oldest manuscript was about A.D. 900, a gap of 1300 years. That was prior to the discovery of the Dead Sea Scrolls. The discovery resulted in manuscripts written between 200 and 30 B.C., shortly before the time of Christ. A complete copy of Isaiah was discovered that dated between 150 and 125 B.C. Old Testament expert, Gleason Archer wrote that the manuscript of Isaiah proved to be 95% identical word for word to the standard Bible. He said that the variations chiefly consisted of slips of the pen and misspellings. (2/58) For instance, Bible experts and authors Norman Geisler and William Nix wrote that of the 166 words in Isaiah 53 only seventeen letters were in question. Ten letters were simply misspellings and four were minor style changes like conjunctions. The remaining three letters spell the word *light* that was added to verse 11 and did not affect the meaning. (2/58) What is the probability after 2,000 years of transmissions that only one word was questioned? The Dead Sea scrolls contained parts or fragments of all the books of the Old Testament except Esther. Archer writes that fragments of the Deuteronomy and Samuel text indicate no differences in doctrine or teaching.

In Chapter 20 we learned that Jesus, the New Testament authors, and early Jewish writers testified on behalf of the Old Testament. The quotes from those reliable witnesses, confirm what we read in today's standard Bible accurately reflects what was written thousands of years ago. No other book of antiquity can make such a claim.

INTERNAL EVIDENCE TEST
(19/41-44 & 2/60-63)

Literary experts follow Aristotle's rule in examining documents. That is, the benefit of doubt goes to the document and not to the critic. In other words, accept the claims of the document. Don't presume unreliability or errors simply because you don't understand or believe the same. The exception is when the author is proven to be wrong or the document contains irrefutable errors and contradictions. The internal test includes the following three parts:

1) What was the primary source of the information? Was the author an eyewitness to the events? This is considered the most reliable source. Did the author receive the information directly from an eyewitness? This is considered the second best source.

2) How close was the primary source in time and geography to the events being recorded? The closer in time and geography the more reliable.

3) When the document was written were there still people alive who could have refuted what was written?

The New Testament was written by eyewitnesses (John, Matthew, James, Jude and Peter) and by those who obtained the information from eyewitnesses (Mark, Luke, and Paul). Every New Testament author lived at the same time and geographical location as the events they wrote about. The New Testament was written and available to be read a short time after the events occurred. There were still a significant number of people living that could have refuted what was written. The New Testament passes the internal test with a five star rating. Many, but not all the Old Testament books pass with a high grade. Unfortunately we don't have the same degree of information about the Old as with the New Testament.

The great historian and physician, Luke wrote (Luke1:1-4), "Many have undertaken to draw up an account of the things that have been fulfilled among us, just as they were handed down to us by those who from the first were eyewitnesses and servants of the word. Therefore, since I myself have carefully investigated everything from the beginning, it seems good also to me to write an orderly account for you, most excellent Theophilus; so that you may know the certainty of the things you have been taught." It is believed that Luke was martyred for his careful investigation and belief.

John, a beloved and trusted follower of Jesus, who assumed responsibility for Jesus' mother when Christ was crucified, wrote (John 20:30-31 and 21:24-25), "Jesus did many other miraculous signs in the presence of his disciples which are not recorded in this book. But these are written that you may believe that Jesus is the Christ, the Son of God, and that by believing you may have life in his name." "This is the disciple who testifies to these things and who wrote them down. We know that his testimony is true. Jesus did many other things as well. If every one of them were written down, I suppose that even the whole world would not have room for the books that would be written." It is believed that there was an attempt on John's life because of his faith. He was one of the few apostles who wasn't martyred, but rather died of natural causes. He did suffer imprisonment and persecution for his beliefs. He lost his brother James to martyrdom.

Peter, the leader among the apostles wrote (II Peter 1:16), "We did not follow cleverly invented stories when we told you about the power and coming of our Lord Jesus Christ, but we were eyewitnesses of his majesty." Peter was martyred for his belief in the truth of Jesus. Tradition relates that Peter was crucified upside down because he didn't feel worthy of being crucified in the same manner as Jesus Christ.

Paul a former persecutor of Christians became a missionary and principle writer of the New Testament. He wrote to the believers in Corinth (Corinthians 15:3-8), "For what I received I passed on to you as of first importance that Christ died for our sins … and was raised on the third day … After that he appeared to more than five hundred of the brothers at the same time, most of whom are still living, though some have fallen asleep … last of all he appeared to me also, as to one abnormally born." Paul was imprisoned twice for his deep faith in Jesus. He was sentenced and martyred during his second time in prison. Universal tradition says he died of decapitation.

When Paul knew death was near ("time has come for my departure") he wrote (II Timothy 4:7), "I have fought a good fight, I have finished the race, I have kept the faith …"

Another important factor confirming the reliability and trustworthiness of the Bible is; although the writers were devout followers they did not conceal incidents that put some of the people and events in bad light. This is highly unusual. If they were providing false accounts about their leaders and related events, they could have easily concealed the negative aspects of the movement. These events include but certainly not limited to:

- The many weaknesses and sins of Old Testament heroes including drunkenness, adultery and murder.
- Peter's fear for his safety resulting in his denial that he was a follower of Jesus.
- The apostles being selfish and competing for higher places in heaven.
- Jesus experiencing such tremendous stress in the garden just prior to his arrest that he actually sweated blood.
- The apostles fleeing and hiding when Jesus was arrested and put to death.
- Jesus' despair in the garden and request to God to lift the requirement of his impending sacrifice through death on a cross.
- Jesus physically demonstrating his anger at the temple money changers.

- The acknowledgment that women were the first witnesses to the resurrection of Jesus. In the Jewish culture of that time women were considered unreliable witnesses. To use women to testify to an event was unthinkable.
- All of the conflicts in the early days of the church as described in Acts and later in Paul's letters.

EXTERNAL EVIDENCE TEST

This test examines other independent material to validate or refute the questioned document. What sources outside the material being tested provides evidence to help authenticate its accuracy and reliability? For very ancient works, this is probably one of the most difficult, yet one of most credible tests.

Early Church leaders (14, 2/63-64 & 19/45)

Second century Church leaders, Bishop Papias of Hierapolis and Bishop Irenaeus of Lyons confirmed the authorship of the four Gospels. They testified that John, an acquaintance of Bishop Papias, wrote his Gospel. Additionally, John relayed that Mark wrote his Gospel based on Peter's teachings, and Matthew addressed his writing to the Jews. John also confirmed that Luke, a student of Paul, wrote his Gospel. (19/45) Irenaeus, Bishop of Lyons in A.D.180 wrote, "So firm is the ground, which these gospels rest that the very heretics themselves bear witness to them ..." (2/63) Ignatius, Bishop of Antioch A.D.

70-110 had gathered enough evidence to confirm the trustworthiness of Scripture. He was so convinced of the Bible's reliability that he was martyred for its truth. It is believed that he was thrown to the lions in the Roman Coliseum. Bishop Polycarp of Smyrna was a disciple of Apostle John. He had complete faith in Jesus and the writings of the apostles. At the age of eighty-six he was put to death for refusing to recant his strong Christian faith. He is believed to have been burned at the stake.

Non-Christian sources (9/77-86)

Josephus, a Pharisee and renowned Jewish historian wrote of the John's baptism and the death of Jesus' half brother, James. He also wrote about Jesus. Tacitus, a Roman historian wrote about the strong faith of the Christians. He said that they were willing to die for their belief in their leader, Christus. He goes on to point out that Jesus was put to death by Pontius Pilate. Pliny the Younger who was governor of Bithynia asked the emperor how to deal with the troublesome Christians who wouldn't renounce Christ. According to Pliny, they honored Christ as if a god. Another historian, Thallus in A.D. 52 tried to explain away the darkness that occurred during the crucifixion of Jesus as simply an eclipse of the sun. The Jewish religious book, the Talmud has passages about Jesus as a false messiah and magician who was justifiably put to death.

Archaeology supports Scriptures
(2/65-67, 4/92-108 & 9/94-108)

Notable Jewish archaeologist Nelson Glueck wrote, "It may be stated categorically that no archaeological discovery has ever controverted a biblical reference." (2/65) Archaeologist William F. Albright of John Hopkins University states, "There can be no doubt that archaeology has confirmed the substantial historicity of Old Testament tradition." (7/72) Sir William Ramsey, respected as one of the premier archaeologists changed his earlier negative reaction to Luke's writings based on archaeology. He concluded the historic accounts in the New Testament were accurate, "Luke is a historian of the first rank ..." (2/70) Archaeologist Joseph Free states, "Archaeology has confirmed countless passages which have been rejected by critics as unhistorical or contradictory to known fact." Classic historian A. N. Sherwin-White writes, "Any attempt to reject its (Acts) basic history even in matters of detail must now appear absurd. Roman historians have long taken it for granted."

Some archaeological examples supporting the Old Testament

- Critics of the Bible claimed that Moses couldn't have written the first five books, because writing didn't exist during that time. In 1901, a large slab of black diorite was discovered that pre dated Moses by three centuries. This slab, seven feet high and six feet wide, contained the detailed laws of Hammurabi

(1792-1750 B.C.). Not only did this discovery provide important background information, but it proved that written language existed hundreds of years prior to Moses. **(12/1259)**

- Bible skeptics asserted that there were no Hittites living during the time of Abraham, thus Genesis in the Old Testament was not accurate. They say that the Hittite era was around 1400-1200 B.C. or at least 500 years after Abraham. In 1906, archaeological finds (The Boghazkoy Tablets) confirmed that the Hittite civilization existed for over 1200 years and during the time of Abraham. (**12/1261 & 19/36**)

- The book of Daniel names Belshazzar as the last king of Babylon. Critics dispute the claim since Babylonian records indicate that Nabonidus was the last king. Besides, outside of the Bible there was no mention of Belshazzar. Archaeology discovered a Babylonian chronicle that reports that King Nabonidus removed himself from his throne for a ten year extended trip to Arabia. He left the kingdom to his eldest son, Belshazzar. Belshazzar was co-regent with his father and remained so until the fall of Babylon. (**7/80 & 11**)

- Daniel writes of Nebuchadnezzar's humble family origin, which critics thought to be inaccurate assuming he was of royal birth. A discovery of an inscription by his father, Nabopolassar revealed that Babylon's greatest

king was "the son of a nobody," which indi-
cates non-royal birth. (4/96)

- Critics cite the victory of Abraham over the
  Mesopotamian kings as recorded in Genesis
  14 and the five cities of the plain as fictitious
  legends. The discovery of the Ebla Tablets in
  the 1960s lists all five cities of the plain and
  confirms the Genesis 14 account related to
  the region. (4/98)

- Archaeology helps confirm the story of
  Joseph's life in Egypt. For example, Joseph
  wanted his bones taken to Canaan whenever
  God restored the land to his people (Genesis).
  Joshua 24:32 records that Joseph's body was
  brought home and buried at Shechem. There
  is a tomb in Shechem considered to be where
  Joseph was buried. A few years before 1960
  this tomb was opened. They discovered a body
  mummified according to Egyptian custom, and
  a number of other Egyptian items including a
  sword used by Egyptian officials. (4/102)

- The list of archaeological discoveries that
  support the accuracy of Old Testament is
  lengthy. Critics are continually proven wrong
  in their bias against the *Word of God* written
  by special men of God. The Dead Sea Scrolls
  discovered in 1947 confirm how faithfully
  and accurately the Jewish scribes made their
  transcription of Scripture.

Some archaeological examples supporting the New Testament

- Sir William Ramsey is a highly respected archaeologist considered one of the best to have ever lived. He disputed the writings of Luke in Acts. He believed they were written in the middle of the second and not the first century. After studying the writings of Luke he stated, "I may fairly claim to have entered on this investigation without prejudice ... On the contrary, I began with a mind unfavorable to it ... more recently I found myself brought into contact with the Book of Acts as an authority for the topography, antiquities and society of Asia Minor ..." He concluded after 30 years of study that, "Luke is a historian of the first rank; not merely are his statements of fact trustworthy ... this author should be placed along with the very greatest of historians." He continues that, "Luke's history is unsurpassed in respect of its trustworthiness." (2/70-71)

- Historians refuted some events that were recorded in the Bible surrounding the birth of Jesus. They claimed there was no census and people did not have to return to their ancestral home. The Bible says Joseph and Mary had to travel to Bethlehem to comply with the mandated census. Archaeological discoveries proved that the Romans had a census every so many years and the entire family was involved. A papyrus found in Egypt confirmed the Roman census, "Seeing that the time has come … it is necessary to compel all those who are residing out of their provinces to return to their homes, that they may carry out the regular order of the census …" (9/101)

- Critics challenged the events surrounding the birth of Jesus. They claimed that Quirinius was not governor of Syria at the time of the birth as Luke wrote. They point out that Quirinius wasn't appointed until A.D. 6 which was after the death of Herod. Luke had to be wrong when he wrote, "… This was the first census taken while Quirinius was the governor of Syria. And all were proceeding to register for the census, everyone to his own city." Archaeologist Jerry Vardaman found a coin showing that Quirinius became governor of Syria in 11 B.C. and remained so until after the death of Herod. (9/101)

- Historians disputed the Bible's claim that Lysanias was ruler of Abilene at the beginning of John the Baptist's ministry in A.D. 27. They claim the only known ruler with the name Lysanias was killed in 36 B.C. However an inscription found near Damascus speaks of Lysanias as the ruler between A.D. 14 and 29. There were two rulers about fifty years apart with the name, Lysanias. (7/82)

- Bible Critics denied that Nazareth existed at the time Jesus allegedly lived there. Their belief is based on the fact that Nazareth is not mentioned in any other ancient writing of that time. Archaeologist found a list showing that after the destruction of Jerusalem in A.D. 70 that a priest relocated to Nazareth. Archaeology also uncovered first century tombs in Nazareth. (9/103)

- Critics felt historical references to Pontius Pilate only existed because he was referred to in the Gospels. That raised some doubt among them that Pilate actually existed. In 1961 archaeologists excavated Caesarea which served as the Roman capital in Palestine. They discovered a 2 X 3 ft inscription in Latin which read, " Pontius Pilate, Prefect of Judea ..." (4/111-112)

Prophecies confirm the uniqueness and reliability of the Bible (2/267-320 & 12/1236-1242)

The Bible is the only book that has confirmed its historical accuracy by fulfilled prophecies. There are over two thousand times that a prophecy was recorded and fulfilled. These prophecies are often very specific including people, events, cities, and nations. False prophets are plentiful even in established religions. Their predictions that remain unfulfilled expose them for what they are. (19/37) Prophecy is not fortunetelling or clairvoyance; there is no guesswork. Notable psychics Jean Dixon and Nostradamus were repeatedly proven wrong in their predictions, or they were so vague that numerous events could have fulfilled their forecasting. The Y-Zine publication, *Who Was the Real Jesus*, reports that according to research and repeated experiments, the success rate of the top psychics is around 1 out of every 10 predictions. Man has been unable to predict specific persons or events in the distant future, with any degree of reliability or consistency. Not so with prophecy! Unlike other forecasting measures, the predictive element of prophecy must occur and be accurate. PH.D Norman L. Geisler, President of Southern Evangelical Seminary and author of over fifty books said, "The Bible is the only book in the world that has precise predictions that were made hundreds of years in advance and that were literally fulfilled." (10/131)

Some Old Testament examples (2/267-320)

* Ezekiel was a prophet of a priestly family from Israel who along with other Jews was exiled to Babylon. He was designated God's spokesman and consultant to the exile leaders. His ministry was from 592-570 B.C. He wrote the Book of Ezekiel which was filled with revelations and prediction about the future. He made prophecies about Judah, Jerusalem, Amon, Moab, Edom, Philistia, Tyre, Sidon, Egypt, and events preceding the restoration of Israel. All of these predictions into the distant future were fulfilled. Ezekiel's prophecy about the City of Tyre as detailed in, "Evidence that Demands a Verdict" by Josh McDowell, is a good example of his God given gift. This prophecy has a number

179

of elements and is recorded in Chapter 26 in the Book of Ezekiel.

Verse seven forecasts that King Nebuchadnezzar would attack Tyre, "For thus says the Lord God, 'Behold, I will bring upon Tyre from the north Nebuchadnezzar king of Babylon, king of kings, with horses, chariots, cavalry, and a great army.'" Three years later Nebuchadnezzar attacked Tyre. After a thirteen year siege, Tyre made a truce and acknowledged Babylonian dominance. However, most of the people fled the mainland to an island a half mile off the Mediterranean coast. They established and fortified the city of Tyre on this island.

Verses three and four predicted the eventual total destruction of Tyre by many nations, "therefore thus says the Lord God, 'Behold, I am against you O Tyre and I will bring many nations against you, as the sea brings up its waves. And they will destroy the walls of Tyre ... and make her a bare rock'" The city was attacked by many nations beginning with Nebuchadnezzar's Babylon, then Alexander the Great's Macedonia (332 B.C.), through the Romans (first century A.D.), to the Christian crusaders (A.D. 1124) and finally the Muslims (A.D. 1291). The city was destroyed by the Muslims in 1291 and never rebuilt. There is a fishing village of Tyre but not at the original site.

Verse fourteen predicts that Tyre will be but a bare rock where fishermen will spread and dry their nets, "And I will make you a bare rock; you will be a place for spreading of nets. You will be built no more …" The mainland of Tyre was reduced to ruins by Alexander the Great over two hundred years after Ezekiel's prediction. Secular historian Philip Myers writes, "… The larger part of the site of the once great city is now bare as the top of a rock – a place where the fishermen that still frequent the spot, spread their nets to dry." (2/276) When Tyre fell in A.D. 1291, it was never rebuilt.

There were seven predictions about Tyre in Ezekiel. Peter W. Stoner, professor of Mathematics in *Science Speaks* writes, "If Ezekiel had looked at Tyre in his day and had made these seven predictions … estimates mean that there would have been only one chance in 75,000,000 of their all coming true. They all came true in the minutest detail." (2/280) Your odds are much better if you, as well as every man, woman and child in California, New York and Texas bought a lottery ticket and you won. Keep in mind this is only one of many prophecies made by Ezekiel. All of which were fulfilled. Other prophets such as Hosea, Micah, Jeremiah, Amos, Nahum and Isaiah also made predictions which where fulfilled.

- Isaiah is probably the best known and most quoted prophet. He, like Ezekiel made a significant number of very specific predictions all of which occurred. An example can be found in the Book of Isaiah. Isaiah 44:28 written about 700 B.C. predicts that a man named Cyrus will declare that Jerusalem will be built and the temple foundation laid. Isaiah writes, "It is I who says of Cyrus, 'He is my shepherd! And he will perform all my desire.' And he declares of Jerusalem, 'She will be built.' And of the temple, 'Your foundation will be laid.'" Chapter 45 continues discussing Cyrus who wouldn't be born for at least another hundred years. At the time of the prophecy in 700 B.C., Jerusalem was fully built and the temple was standing. One hundred and fourteen years later in 586 B.C. Nebuchadnezzar destroyed both the city of Jerusalem and its temple. Forty-seven years after that the Persians conquered Jerusalem, a Persian king named Cyrus gave a decree to rebuild the temple in Jerusalem. This was about 161 years after the prophecy. (4/56-57)

A modern illustration of this prophecy would be as if in 1785, one of our founding fathers predicted that Harry S. Truman would help restore England after World War II and rebuild the Canterbury Cathedral.

New Testament examples of fulfilled prophecies
(12/1236-1242)

Theologians cite from 200 to 300 Old Testament prophecies about the Messiah that were fulfilled hundreds of years later in the person of Jesus Christ.

Some of these appear somewhat vague, but there is general agreement that there are at least 60 major messianic prophecies. However, much like finger-prints, it should only take a match of eight non- refutable prophecies to confirm the accuracy, reliability and uniqueness of the Bible. Some of the more common and easily understood messianic prophecies are:

1) John the Baptist: The prophecy in Isaiah 40:3 called for John the Baptist to pave the way for Jesus, "A voice is calling, 'clear the way for the Lord in the wilderness ...'" Malachi 3:1 also predicted John as the forerunner, "Behold I am going to send My messenger and he will clear the way before Me ..."

The fulfillment of this prophecy can be found in Matthew 3:1-3, "... John the Baptist came preaching in the wilderness of Judea saying, 'Repent, for the kingdom of heaven is at hand. For this is the one referred to by Isaiah the prophet saying, 'The voice of one crying in the wilderness, make ready the way of the Lord ...'" Luke 1:17 records the following, "And it is he [John the Baptist] who will go as a forerunner before Him in the spirit and power of Elijah ..." Luke 7:27 records Jesus as saying, "This is the one [John the Baptist] about whom it is written, 'I will send my messenger ahead of you, who will prepare your way before you.'" (NI)

2) Messiah born in Bethlehem: The prophet Micah forecast that the Messiah would be born in the city of Bethlehem. Micah 5:2 says, "But as for you Bethlehem Ephrathah, too little to be among the clans of Judah, from you One will go forth for Me to be ruler in Israel. His going forth is from long ago, from the days of eternity."

Matthew and Luke confirm the prophecy was fulfilled in that Jesus was born in Bethlehem. Matthew 2:1 reads, "Now after Jesus was born in Bethlehem of Judea ..."

3) Messiah born of a virgin: Isaiah predicted in 7:14 that the Messiah would be born of a virgin, "Therefore the Lord Himself will give you a sign: Behold, a virgin will be with child and bear a son, and she will call His name Immanuel [God with us]."

Luke provides the details on this prediction being fulfilled in Chapter 1:26-38, "... and the virgin's name was Mary ... And the angel said to her, '... And behold you will conceive in your womb and bear a son ...' And Mary said to the angel, 'How can this be, since I am a virgin?' The angel answered and said to her, 'The Holy Spirit will come upon you ... for that reason the holy offspring shall be called the Son of God.'" The virgin Mary subsequently gave birth to Jesus in Bethlehem.

4) Messiah comes out of Egypt: Hosea prophesied in Chapter 11:1 that the Messiah would come out of Egypt, "When Israel was a youth I loved him, and out of Egypt I called My son."

This was fulfilled when the holy family was told to flee from Judea to Egypt in order to avoid King Herod's wrath. The family remained there until Herod's death when they returned to Israel. This is recorded in Matthew 2:14, "And he [Joseph] arose and took the Child [Jesus] and his mother [Mary] by night and departed for Egypt; and was there until the death of Herod."

5) Messiah's ministry in Galilee: Isaiah predicted that the Messiah's ministry would center around the Province of Galilee. In Chapter 9:1-2 he writes, " … He shall make it glorious, by the way of the sea, on the other side of Jordan, Galilee of the Gentiles …"

It is well documented that Jesus' ministry was primarily in the region of Galilee around the Sea of Galilee. Mark's Gospel Chapter 1:14 says, "… Jesus came into Galilee preaching the Gospel of God." The apostle, Judas was the only one of the twelve apostles not from Galilee.

6) Messiah to make a triumphal entry into Jerusalem on a donkey: Zechariah made a prophecy that the Messiah would make a great entry into Jerusalem humbly riding on a donkey. He wrote in Chapter 9:9 of his Old Testament book, "Rejoice greatly, O daughter of Zion! Shout in triumph, O daughter of Jerusalem! Behold, your king is coming to you; He is just and endowed with salvation, humble, and mounted on a donkey, even on a colt, the foal of a donkey."

Toward the end of his ministry Jesus openly entered Jerusalem, home of his enemies, the Jewish leaders. He rode in on a donkey's colt to a cheering crowd. Christians celebrate this event as Palm Sunday. Mark records the event in Chapter 11:1-11, "And as they approached Jerusalem … And they brought the colt to Jesus and put their garments on it; and He sat upon it. And many spread their garments in the road, and others spread leafy branches which they cut from the fields … were crying out, 'Hosanna! Blessed is He who comes in the name of the Lord … Hosanna in the highest.' And He entered Jerusalem …"

7) Betrayed by a friend: The writer of Psalms 41 predicted that the Messiah would be betrayed by a close friend. Verse 9 reads, "Even my close friend in whom I trusted, who ate my bread, has lifted his heal against me."

The Gospels relay that the apostle Judas betrayed his leader which led to the arrest and subsequent death of Jesus. Mark14:18 reads, "And as they were reclining at the table and eating, Jesus said, 'Truly I say to you that one of you will betray Me, one who is eating with Me.'" John 18:2 records, "Now Judas also, who was betraying Him, knew the place; for Jesus had often met there with His disciples."

8) Betrayed for thirty pieces of silver: Zechariah prophesied that Jesus would be betrayed for thirty pieces of silver. He wrote in Chapter 11:12, "And

I said to them, '… give me my wages …' So they weighed out thirty shekels of silver as my wage." Matthew 26:14-15 reports that, "… Judas Iscariot went to the chief priests and said, 'What are you willing to give me to deliver Him up to you?' and they weighed out to him thirty pieces of silver."

9) Pierced and scourged for our sins: Isaiah predicted that the Messiah would be pierced and scourged [whipped] for our sins. He wrote in 53:5, "But He was pierced through for our transgressions … And by His scourging we are healed." The Gospels report that Jesus died for our sins. They describe the events leading to his death as both being scourged and nailed (pierced) to the cross. Mark 15:15 relates, "And wishing to satisfy the multitude, Pilate released Barabbas for them, and after having Jesus scourged, he delivered Him to be crucified."

10) The Messiah would be sneered at and mocked: The writer of Psalm: 22 forecast that the Messiah would be sneered at and mocked to have God save him. Verses 7 and 8 read, "All who see me sneer at me, … they wag the head, saying, 'Commit yourself to the Lord; let Him deliver him; let Him rescue him …'" Matthew reports in 27:39-43, "And those passing by were hurling abuse at Him, wagging their heads … In the same way the chief priests, along with the scribes and elders were mocking Him, and saying: '… He trusts in God; Let Him deliver Him now if He takes pleasure in Him; for He said: I am the Son of God.'"

These ten examples are a sample of the numerous Old Testament prophecies fulfilled by Jesus Christ. "The Open Bible" edition of the *New American Standard Bible* summarizes forty-four prophecies. Josh McDowell's book "Evidence that Demands a Verdict" summarizes sixty-one prophecies fulfilled by Christ. Many of the prophecies from these two sources were the same, but there were some that were different. Additional prophecies include, but certainly not limited to, Jesus' bones wouldn't be broken, Jesus would be offered gall and vinegar, the soldiers would cast lots for his clothes, he would cry out that he was forsaken, and darkness would cover the land.

The above represents some prophecies from the Old Testament that were fulfilled 500-700 years later in the New Testament. The possibility of only eight of these prophecies being fulfilled in just one man is 1 in 10 to the 17th or 1 in 100,000,000,000,000,000.

Math expert Peter Stoner best illustrates visually what this means. He describes the possibilities mathematically by imagining silver dollars spread across the entire state of Texas two feet deep. He then would mark only one silver dollar mixing it in with the others covering 266,874 square miles. This is about 774 miles east to west and 737 miles north to south. He then suggests blindfolding a man and telling him to travel the state of Texas wherever he wishes. At some time the blindfolded man must select a silver dollar. What is the chance that he would pick the marked dollar? About the same as prophets, based solely on their own human abilities, projecting eight specific prophecies and having them fulfilled through one man.(2/67)

It would be difficult to conclude from the evidence that these and the other prophecies were not guided by a Supreme Being. It would be equally difficult to conclude, considering all the evidence, that the Bible is unreliable and not one-of-a-kind. An objective jury would no doubt convict the Bible as being accurate and trustworthy. The evidence is in and the case closed. However, the reference books have much more evidence. This chapter only represents a summary of the material compiled by the true experts and scholars.

REVIEW

1) What does the term "unique" mean?
2) List the reasons why the Bible is unique.
3) What is the study of the reliability of ancient documents called?
4) Explain the bibliographical test and its components.
5) Explain the internal test and its components.
6) Explain the external test and its components.
7) How does the Bible compare when applying these tests? Give some specifics.
8) How much of a corruption rate exists between New Testament manuscripts and the current Bible? Can you give that in terms of numbers?

9) There are approximately how many quotes from the New Testament by early church leaders? Why is this important?
10) Why are the Dead Sea Scrolls important in relationship to the bibliographical test?
11) What in your opinion are the most compelling factors confirming the accuracy and reliability of the Bible?
12) Give examples where archaeology supports the Old and New Testament.
13) Give examples where prophecy supports the Old and New Testament.

CHAPTER 22

CRITICS QUESTION THE BIBLE

—∿∿—

The Bible has been and continues to be the most critiqued, scrutinized, and criticized book ever written. There are people who spend a lifetime trying to disprove even minor passages in the Bible. There are times when they believe they have found an error or contradiction only to be proven wrong. It has already been demonstrated that archaeology has not found anything to invalidate the claims of the Bible. New archaeological findings continue to confirm the accuracy of both the Old and New Testament. It has also been demonstrated that the fulfilled prophecies support the trustworthiness of the Bible. One area not yet examined when considering the reliability of the Bible is the alleged contradictions within the Bible.

Critics carefully review the text of the Bible looking for any errors or contradictions. When they find what appears to be a mistake they immediately indict the entire book. They don't apply the standard of justice that says, "Innocent until proven guilty."

The burden of proof is on the critic not the book. The rule of literary criticism is to give the benefit of the doubt to the document. All literary works should be measured by the same standard. Varying descriptions of the same event are not necessarily a contradiction. In fact it tends to add credibility to the record since witnesses rarely describe the same event in a similar manner.

The question to answer before examining alleged contradictions is, "what is a contradiction?" The rule for contradiction spells out that, something can't be both an "X" and a "non-X" at the same time. In other words Jesus couldn't have died on a cross both in Jerusalem and Bethlehem at the same time. Most Biblical scholars don't believe there are any true contradictions in the Bible. They have repeatedly demonstrated that there are reasonable explanations for difficult passages in the Old and New Testament. Careful examination of what critics claim to be contradictions prove not to be the case. Below are some examples:

Wasn't Jesus wrong when he predicted the generation to see his return?

In Luke 21, Jesus describes to the apostles the events leading up to his return and second coming. He then says, "Truly, I say to you, this generation will not pass away until all things take place." Critics of the Bible point out that the apostle's generation did pass away before those things occurred. Reading the passage carefully, it is likely that Jesus was referring to the generation that was alive at the beginning of the events signaling the return of Jesus. He was not referring to the apostle's generation or the first century A.D. Jesus compares the signs as "birth pangs." He states that the generation existing at the beginning of the "birth pangs" will be alive to witness the promised, "delivery"

What about the discrepancies between the genealogies of Jesus in Matthew 1:1-17 and Luke 3:23-38? (6/60-61 & 27/168)

Critics point out that the two Biblical genealogies of Jesus have significant differences. It is true that both accounts have differences. Matthew was reflecting Joseph's lineage. Joseph, the adoptive father would have been the legal ancestor through whom Jesus' *royal lineage* would have been traced. Matthew says, "and to Jacob was born Joseph the husband of Mary." It is believed that Luke traced the genealogy through Mary's ancestry, which would be Jesus' *human lineage*. Luke says, "Jesus ... being supposedly the son of Joseph, the son of Heli." In the Jewish culture, women were considered second class, thus it was common practice to only mention the man's name. Luke acknowledges that Jesus is not the son of Joseph both here and when he writes of the virgin birth. He may very well be saying that Joseph was the son-in-law of Heli (Mary's father). The other possibility is Luke's assumption that since God, not Joseph, is the true father that the lineage has to be that of Mary. Both the lineages in Matthew and Luke converge at the same point. They confirm that Jesus was a descendant of David, legally through his step-father and by blood through his mother.

Another possibility suggested was they were both Joseph's lineage with one being legal and the other human. Under Jewish practice if in following the family line someone didn't have a direct offspring the Jews would raise up legal heirs through various practices. This problem of tracing was made even more difficult because some names are omitted which was an acceptable standard of the ancient world.

Matthew 8:5-10 says the centurion asked Jesus for a healing whereas Luke 7:1-10 says the elders or friends asked. (9/46)

Critics say in reading the passages that this difference is an unresolved conflict. On the surface that may appear to be true. A closer examination of the two accounts resolves any perceived conflict. Matthew describes interaction between the centurion and Jesus over healing the centurion's slave. He doesn't describe how the centurion first came into contact with Jesus other than at some point "a centurion came to Him". Luke says that the centurion sent elders asking Jesus to come. Luke then goes on to say Jesus headed for the house and the centurion sent friends. Based on the dialogue, the centurion must have accompanied his friends to meet with Jesus. The dialogue described in both Matthew and Luke is similar and no doubt directly from the centurion. He said that he didn't feel worthy to have Jesus come "under my roof." He then acknowledged Jesus' authority by saying, "... For I too am a man under authority with soldiers under me ..." Based on the centurion's own words as described in both Gospels, it is plain that he directly asked Jesus to heal his servant.

Mark 5 describes Jesus casting the demon into swine at Gerasa (Gerasene) whereas Matthew 8:28-34 says it happened in Gadara (Gadarenes). (9/46-47)

Critics point out that this same event could not have occurred in two different cities, thus there is a definite contradiction. There has been some confusion as to the correct site. However, the reference is to the "country of the Gerasene" and the "country of the Gadarenes" not to a specific city. The Gerasene and Gadarenes were the people. Geography and history shows that both territories probably overlapped therefore both accounts could have been right.

Archaeology discovered the ruins of a town on the Eastern shore of the Sea of Galilee pronounced Khersa which translated into Greek is Gerasa. It very well could have been rendered in Greek as Gerasa in the Province of Gadara.

How could Moses have written Deuteronomy since it gives an account of his death? (6/22)

Critics say that a man cannot write accounts of his own death thus Moses didn't write Deuteronomy. Deuteronomy is a farewell address of Moses to the Israelites in the plains of Moab. However, he couldn't have written about his own death as related in the last chapter (34). It is believed that Moses wrote the first 33 chapters and Joshua (mentioned in Chapter 34) wrote the last one. It was common practice that an obituary be placed at the conclusion of the last work of a great author. It would have been more suspect if, since Moses' life was told so specifically, that his death wasn't recorded at the end of his final work.

Contradiction in accounts of Siseras' death. (4/127)

Critics say that Judges 5:25-27 describes that Sisera was drinking milk when Jael killed him, whereas Judges 4:21 says that Sisera was sleeping when he was killed. Careful reading of Judges 5:25-27 does not say he was drinking milk at the moment he was killed. Rather Jael gave him milk instead of water prior to driving a tent peg into his temple. Sisera very well could have fallen asleep after drinking the milk. In fact, the milk could have been laced with a sedative.

Paul's conversion accounts differ in relationship to what his companions heard. (4/128)

Critics point out in Acts 9:7 the men with Paul at his conversion "heard a voice" whereas Acts 22:9 states, "they heard not the voice of him that spoke to me." This is definitely a contradiction. Either they heard or they didn't. It can't be both.

Greek text uses two different forms of the Greek verb, "to hear". One (Acts 9:7) simply expresses sounds being heard but not whether the person understands those sounds. Like hearing a rap song but not having a clue as what is being said. The other is the accusative form (Acts 22:9) and describes a hearing that could include understanding the words.

In Acts 22:9, Luke isn't saying they didn't hear certain sounds but rather they didn't hear in such a way as they understood what was being said.

Thus in Acts 22:9 they did not hear a voice they understood and in Acts 9:7 they heard a sound but didn't understand it. Both are saying the same thing.

Two different accounts of how Judas died. (6/84-85)

Critics are quick to point out that Matthew 27:5 says Judas hung himself, whereas Luke in Acts 1:18 says Judas fell headlong and burst open. Which is it? It is probable that Judas died hanging himself with his girdle on a tree branch near the edge of a cliff overlooking Hinnom. After some time either the cloth could have ripped, become untied or possibly the branch could have snapped thrusting the bloated Judas headfirst down a cliff; bursting open on impact. This is consistent with the Hinnom terrain. The Hinnom valley has a jagged rocky floor and trees grow around the ledge of the cliff above the valley. The drop is from 25 to 40 feet.

Number of animals in Noah's ark is not plausible. (6/89)

Critics laugh at the idea of fitting all those animals in a boat. They say this story is consistent with mythology and not possible. Whether you want to believe the literal story (Genesis chapters six through eight) or not is your choice, but it was possible. The Bible goes so far as to give the dimensions of the ship. The ark was 437.5 feet long, 72.92 feet wide and 43.75 feet high with three decks. This would provide approximately 95,700 sq. feet of space. The load capacity of the ark would be equal to 522 standard railroad stock cars. Each stock car can carry 240 sheep, thus the ark could have handled 125,000 sheep.

Experts estimate that during Noah's time there were approximately 17,600 species of animals that would need protection from the flood. The Bible says Noah was to take a male and female of each unclean animal and seven including a male and female of each clean animal (estimated at 50% of the total animals). This means the ark, which could handle 125,000 sheep, would have to hold 79,000 animals. Most of the 17,600 species would be much smaller than sheep. The ark would have room for the animals plus food, supplies and living quarters. It was possible! Not that I would want to be a passenger.

Jesus was wrong when he said mustard seed was the smallest. (27/165)

Critics have make comments about Jesus' lack of agricultural knowledge. They cite Matthew 13:31-32 when Jesus said that the mustard seed was, "… the smallest of all seeds …" They point out that actually an orchid and a petunia seed is smaller. Was the Son of God wrong or misquoted? The answer is neither. The word that Jesus used for seed was actually a garden seed men plant to grow crops. He even infers that when he says it grows into the, "largest of garden crops and becomes a tree." The black mustard seed which was common in that region was the smallest of the crop seeds. The black mustard plant grew from ten to fifteen feet with a thick main trunk and branches able to hold the weight of a bird. Jesus said, "… where birds can come and find shelter in its branches."

Jonah living in a whale is a fable. (6/96-97 & 26)

Critics challenge as impossible a man living in a whale for three days and nights. The Bible in Jonah 1:17 relates that Jonah was swallowed by a "great" fish and remained inside it's "stomach" for three days and nights. Could this have occurred? Maybe! Was the story an allegory or hyperbole? Maybe! However, there were and are certain species of whale ("great fish") capable of swallowing a man whole. Some have been known to swallow animals larger than man. This includes certain whales, whale shark, white shark and sperm shark.

It is alleged that in 1891 a whaling ship, Star of the East lost a man named James Bartly who was thrown overboard. Subsequently a whale was killed and brought along the ship's side for cleaning. After a day and a half the crew discovered Bartly doubled up and unconscious inside the whale. They revived him and he lived. His hands and face were bleached white and skin wrinkled from the gastric juices in the whale. Apparently the anatomy of these animals could provide sufficient oxygen for survival. (26)

Were there one or two blind men at Jericho?

Critics point out the contradiction in Gospel accounts of the number of blind men at Jericho. Two

Gospels say there was one man and another says there were two men. Luke 18:35-42 and Mark 10:46-52 describe the event as Jesus healing one blind man. Matthew 20:29-34 describes two men being healed of blindness.

Is this a contradiction? No. It is simply different accounts of the same event from different views. Neither Luke nor Mark said there was only one blind man. Varying descriptions of the same event are not contradictions.

For instance, assume you saw your company's Chief Executive Officer and a state senator having lunch together and told a friend that you saw the two of them. Later you were talking to another friend and told that friend you saw your the CEO having lunch. Is that a contradiction? Are you lying? No, you just relayed the event differently to two people for what could be a variety of reasons. If you told the second friend that you only saw the CEO and not the senator then you would be lying or making a contradictory statement.

These two Biblical descriptions fall into the same category. There were two men, however Luke and Mark chose to focus on only one. Mark even knew the one's name.

Were there one or two angels at the tomb? (1/25)

Critics say the Gospels contradict each other regarding how many angels were at the tomb. Matthew 28:2 describes one angel at the tomb where Jesus was buried. John doesn't say anything about an angel and Luke 24:4 describes two angels. Is this a contradiction? No. It is just different accounts of the same event from three different views. Matthew didn't say there was only one angel and John didn't say there were no angels. In fact John gives a much abbreviated version of the visit to the tomb and not with the same emphasis as the others.

There are two different times cited as to when Jesus was hung on the cross. (6/44-45)

Critics cite the difference between Mark and John concerning the time Jesus was crucified as a major contradiction. Mark 15:25 says it was the third hour when they crucified him. John 19:14 states it was about the sixth hour when he was condemned and delivered to be crucified. A three-hour difference is a conflict.

It is probable that John was using a different method of describing time than Mark.

The Romans calculated the day from midnight to midnight much like the military. To them the sixth hour would have been 0600 hours or 6 a.m. That is the time John says the trial ended. This would give plenty of time (three hours) for the activities that preceded the actual crucifixion to take place by 9 a.m., the time cited by Mark. He was using the Jewish method of measuring time. The Jewish day was from sunset to sunset divided into eight equal parts. The first morning watch in Jewish time was 6 a.m. to 9 a.m. That would make nine in the morning the third hour.

REVIEW

1. If the Bible is accurate, how do you explain all the contradictions?
2. Explain the two different genealogies of Jesus as recorded in Matthew and Luke.
3. How could Moses have written Deuteronomy when it contains the account of his death?
4. How do you explain the different accounts of how Judas committed suicide?
5. How could all those animals have fit in Noah's Ark?
6. Was Jesus wrong when he said the mustard seed was the smallest?
7. Explain the difference between Matthew's account that there was only one angel at the tomb and Luke who wrote that there were two?
8. How do you explain there being two different times recorded as to when Jesus was hung on the cross? Mark says the third hour whereas John says it was the sixth hour.

CHAPTER 23

DID JESUS REALLY LIVE?

—⁓—

V ery few people refute the fact that Jesus Christ lived during the first century A.D. However, there are a few skeptics who ask, "How do you know Jesus really lived and was not just a mythical character like other so-called gods?" The fact that the majority of people including leaders of non-Christian religions, historians, world leaders, atheists and agnostics believe that Jesus actually lived is compelling testimony to his existence. In order to doubt Jesus lived, a person, if consistent, would probably question all ancient history. The evidence supporting the existence of Jesus is overwhelming and consists of three major sources.

The New Testament

Evidence has been presented earlier in this book that the Bible is an accurate and reliable source. The twenty-seven books that make up the New Testament testify to the fact that Jesus lived in first century Israel and died a horrible death. Jesus is the main character of the New Testament. The Bible gives very specific details about his life including dates, times, people, places, events, and even his words. The New Testament specifically names his parents, relatives, friends, followers, and enemies, as well as place of birth and death. If false, all of this information could have been easily examined and refuted.

Many who wrote the New Testament were eyewitnesses. Almost all of these eyewitnesses and many other followers died for their belief in Jesus. The twenty-seven books were written when believing and non-believing witnesses still lived. If untrue, the non-believing Jews and Romans could have rebutted the accounts of Jesus. There are no documents from that time that claimed Jesus was a myth and didn't exist. In fact just the opposite is true. There were many first and second century Christian and non-Christian sources that mentioned Jesus Christ.

Early Christian leaders (28/26-42)

Early church leaders confirmed the existence of Jesus Christ. This was during a time (second century) that was close enough to the life of Jesus that they could have been challenged. A few of these leaders include:

Tertullian, leader in the Carthage Church who lived from A.D. 160 to 220 was converted to Christianity. He challenged those who denied the deity of Christ.

Clement, leader of the church at Rome around A.D. 90 wrote of Jesus Christ in a letter to the Corinth Church.

Clement of Alexandria lived from approximately A.D. 160 to 212. He was the head of a Christian school and wrote of Jesus while countering Gnostic philosophers.

Ignatius, the Bishop of Antioch wrote a number of letters about Jesus in about A.D. 115 knowing that he had been condemned to death. He was martyred for Jesus.

Polycarp, leader of the church at Smyrna lived from A.D. 70 to 150. He was a student of the apostle John and teacher of Iraneous. Polycarp was a prolific writer who often referenced Jesus. He was martyred for his faith.

Justin, a second century apologist was martyred in A.D. 166. He was a Samaritan who was converted to Christianity. Justin wrote against the Jewish attack on Jesus.

Non-Christian sources (2/81-87)

Cornelius Tacitus, a Roman historian in A.D. 112 wrote about Nero. He believed that Nero was responsible for the burning of Rome. He wrote that Nero, "... punished with the most exquisite tortures the person commonly called Christians, who were hated ... Christus, the founder of the name was put to death by Pontius Pilate ..."

Lucian of Samosata, a second century satirist spoke negatively of Christ and the Christian. He indicted Christ as, "... the man who was crucified in Palestine because he introduced this new cult into the world ..."

Flavius Josephus born in A.D. 37 was a renowned Jewish historian and Pharisee. He wrote, "Now there was about this time Jesus, a wise man. For he was one who wrought surprising feats and was a teacher of such people as accept the truth gladly. He won over many Jews and many of the Greek. When Pilate, upon hearing him accused by men of the highest standing among us, had condemned him to be cruci-fied, those who had in the first place come to love him did not give up their affection for him. And the tribe of Christians, so called after him, has still to this day not disappeared." (9/79-80) He also wrote, "... and brought before it the brother of Jesus the so-called Christ, whose name was James, ..."

Suetonius, a Roman historian in A.D. 120 wrote, "As the Jews were making constant disturbances at the instigation of Chrestus [another spelling of Christus or Christ], he expelled them from Rome."

Pliny the Younger, a governor in Asia Minor in A.D. 112 wrote to the emperor seeking advice in how to treat Christians. He wrote that genuine Christians couldn't be induced to curse Christ. He said, "... they sang in alternate verse a hymn to Christ as to a god ..."

Thallus, a Samaritan historian was one of the first Gentiles to write of Jesus (A.D. 52). He explained away the darkness that occurred when Jesus died as an eclipse of the sun.

Mara Bar Serapion, who was in prison around A.D. 73, wrote a letter to encourage his son try to acquire wisdom. He noted that those who persecuted the wise men like Socrates, Pythagoras and Christ experienced misfortune. He asks, "… What advantage did the Jews gain from executing their wise King? It was just after that that their kingdom was abolished [A.D. 70] …"

REVIEW

1. What are the three main sources used to confirm that Jesus actually existed?
2. Name a few of the early Christian leaders who wrote about Jesus?
3. Name a few non-Christians whose writings confirmed that Jesus actually lived?

CHAPTER 24

JESUS IS GOD AND THE PROMISED MESSIAH

—⁓—

Jesus said he was God
(2/104)

Two options_

The claim was false (He really isn't God)	The claim was true (He is God)
Two options	Two options

He knew his claim was false	He didn't know his claim was false	Accept Him	Reject Him
He was a liar, fool, and evil	He was deluded and severely mentally ill		

One of life's most important questions to ask and try to answer is, who was Jesus Christ? Because of the potential ramifications, it behooves everyone to carefully examine this issue, and try to reach a decision. Spiritually, it could be a life and death question. Was Jesus the God and Savior that billions of people over the last two thousand years claimed and many died for? Non-Christians generally believe that Jesus was a good moral man who was one of history's greatest religious leaders. They say he ranks in the same category as Abraham, Moses, Mohammed, Buddha, and other great religious leaders. These are all very complimentary comments and most would be honored.

However, Jesus was different and unique among the recognized religious leaders. None of them professed to be God. Neither Mohammed, Moses, Buddha, Confucius, Peter, nor Paul, or their followers, ever claimed or even insinuated they were deity. Jesus Christ and his followers did make that declaration. They convinced a large portion of the world's population that he was God and the Savior. How does a person decide whether Jesus was God, or simply a good moral religious leader? That process can begin by examining the available options using logic and deductive reasoning. The first issue to resolve is who did Jesus say he was? The answer is clear. He didn't say he was a god or was like a god as some kings believed about themselves. He stated emphatically that he was God and the promised Messiah. He was the one and only God, the giver of life. That narrows the available options to consider down to two; either his claim was true or his claim was false.

TRUE: If his claim was true then there are two alternatives from which to choose. That is to either accept him or reject him as your God and Savior.

FALSE: If his claim was false then there are only two alternatives to consider. The first is that he knew he wasn't God and made deliberate false assertions. The other is that he didn't know that his claim was false and thought he was God. If you chose the first then you have to conclude that Jesus was a liar, hypocrite, and a fool since he died for that lie. If you chose the second then you have to conclude that Jesus was deluded and mentally ill.

NEITHER: There is no neutral ground. He can't be a good moral religious leader and also a liar or lunatic. Which is it? Examine the options and try to determine which is most logical.

Jesus said he was God and the Messiah
(2/89-109 & 9/131-143)

Did Jesus claim he was God and the promised Messiah? Critics argue that Jesus never said with certainty that he was God or the Messiah. Some say that his apostles created his deity after his death. Others say that the early church made that pronouncement, while still others say that Roman Emperor Constantine and the Council at Nicaea made that declaration. This is the critical issue to resolve. What does the evidence show?

- Mark 14:61-64 records portions of Jesus' trial. The high priest questioned Jesus, "Are you the Christ, the Son of the blessed One?" Jesus answered, "I am and you shall see the Son of Man sitting at the right hand of Power and coming with the clouds of Heaven." That was all the high priest needed to confirm his charge that this Jesus was guilty of blasphemy by claiming to be God.

- Matthew 26:64 seems to give a slightly different response from Jesus to this question by the high priest. Jesus responded, "You have said it yourself ..." That may appear an evasive answer but in those days, *Thou Sayest* was the traditional method in which an educated Jew replied to an important question. Courtesy would not allow a direct yes or no. Obviously the Jewish leader had no problem understanding his answer to be; Yes, I'm God and the Messiah. (2/91)

- Luke 22:70 records the response as, "Yes, I am." No matter which Gospel you reference the answer is the same. There is no contradiction. Jesus was asked and he answered that he was God.

- In the trial before Pilate, Jesus was asked, "Are you the king of the Jews?" He answered, "It is as you say" as recorded in Matthew, Mark and Luke. John goes into more detail and includes Jesus making such confirming statements as, "My kingdom is not of this world ..." and "You say correctly that I am a king ..."

- The Jewish leaders confirmed that Jesus claimed to be God. While he hung on the cross the leaders were mocking him and saying among other things "... for He Said, 'I am the Son of God.'" (Matthew 27:43). When the crowd yelled out for Pilate to crucify him they said, "... He ought to die because he made himself out to be the Son of God." (John 19:7)

- In John 10:30-33 the apostle recalls a confrontation between Jesus and some Jews. Jesus said, "I and My Father are one." The Jews wanted to stone him for blasphemy because, "You being a man make yourself out to be God."

- John 8:58 quotes Jesus speaking to the Jews, "Truly, truly, I say to you before Abraham was born, I AM." The Jews understood what he just said and picked up stones to throw at him. Jesus said he lived before the Father (Abraham) of the Jewish nation. To the Jews this meant he was the same as Jehovah who exists eternally. He also said he was God by using, *I AM*. Moses asked God what he should say when the sons of Israel ask who sent him. God answered, "I AM Who I AM ... Thus you shall say to the sons of Israel, I AM has sent me to you." (Exodus 3:13-14)

- Matthew 16:15-17 records Peter's famous affirmation of Jesus as God and the Messiah.

Jesus asked the apostles, "But who do you say I am?" Peter answered, "Thou art the Christ, the Son of the living God." If that were not true Jesus would have rebuked him. Instead he responded, "Blessed are you, Simon Barjona [Peter] because flesh and blood did not reveal this to you but My Father who is in heaven." He also warned the apostles at that time they were not to reveal he was the Christ, which means the Anointed One, Savior and Messiah. Doubting Thomas affirmed Jesus' deity when he said (John 20:28), "My Lord and My God." Jesus did not correct him for calling him Lord and God.

- Jesus referred to himself as the *Son of Man* with that title occurring 82 times in the Gospels. Jesus clearly identified himself as the one about whom Daniel prophesied (Daniel 7:13-14), "… One like a Son of Man was coming …" The term *Son of Man* also confirms the human side of Jesus and his lineage to David. This was a title those he ministered to could relate. The term, *Son of Man* reflects both his humanity and his deity.

- The Samaritan woman at the well (John 4) said to Jesus, "I know that Messiah is coming (He who is called Christ) …" Jesus responded, "I who speak to you am He."

- There are a number of passages in the Gospels where Jesus forgave people of their sins. This greatly upset the Jewish leaders since under their law only God could forgive sins. Mark 2:7 records the Jewish leaders' response to Jesus, "Why does this man speak that way? He is blaspheming, who can forgive sins but God alone?"

- John, one of the apostles closest to Jesus, was with him the entire three years. He wrote at the beginning of his Gospel, "In the beginning was the Word [Jesus] and the Word [Jesus] was with God and the Word [Jesus] was God ...."

- The apostle Philip in the last days of Jesus' ministry was still confused. John 14:7-10 relays the following interaction between Philip and Jesus. Philip says, "Lord, show us the Father and it is good enough for us." Jesus responds, "Have I been so long with you and yet you have not come to know me, Philip? He who has seen me has seen the Father, how do you say, 'Show us the Father?'..."

There are many other examples supporting the fact that Jesus declared he was God and the promised Messiah. His closest followers certainly believed Jesus and most died for that belief. His enemies were convinced that Jesus professed to be God, and had him put to death for that unthinkable blasphemy. Even a Roman soldier at the death of Jesus said, "Truly this man was the Son of God." The evidence is conclusive that Jesus believed himself to be God and the Messiah.

There is however one more issue to resolve concerning Jesus' identity. Did Jesus fulfill the Old Testament prophecies about the Messiah? He said he fulfilled the prophecies, but is there any support for that claim? There were at least sixty messianic prophecies in the Old Testament. These predictions were made hundreds of years before the birth and life of Jesus Christ. The Messiah was to be the Savior sent by God for the redemption of mankind. If Jesus didn't fulfill these prophecies then he couldn't be the Christ. An examination of the evidence can determine whether he passed the test. Jesus repeatedly said that he was the Messiah and came to fulfill the prophecies. Some examples confirming this assertion were already covered in the preceding pages. Additional references include the following quotes from Jesus:

- Luke 24:44, "… that all things which are written about me in the Law of Moses and the Prophets and the Psalms must be fulfilled."
- John 5:46, "For if you believe Moses, you would believe me: for he wrote of me."
- Matthew 5:17, "Do not think that I came to abolish the Law or the Prophets; I did not come to abolish, but to fulfill."
- Matthew 26:56, during his arrest Jesus told Peter not to resist and said, "… But all this has taken place that the Scriptures of the Prophets may be fulfilled."
- Luke 4:21-22, Jesus began his public ministry at the synagogue by reading out of Isaiah about the Messiah. When He finished the

reading He said, "Today this Scripture has been fulfilled in your hearing."

Did Jesus fulfill the prophecies about the Savior as he professed? Some theologians cite between 200 and 300 Old Testament prophecies that were fulfilled hundreds of years later in the person of Jesus. Some of these appear somewhat vague, but there is general agreement that there are at least 60 major messianic prophecies. However, it should only take eight, like matching loops and whorls in fingerprints to present conclusive proof that Jesus was the Messiah prophesized in the Old Testament. The odds that eight prophecies would be fulfilled in one man are 1 in 10 to the 17th (1 in 100,000,000,000,000,000). Given those odds, it would be hard to conclude that Jesus wasn't the predicted Messiah. Can you imagine the odds if the eight were doubled to sixteen prophecies or as many as sixty?

Most believe Jesus fulfilled the sixty prophecies. Chapter 21 describes ten of these prophecies in some detail. They include: 1) Preceded by a forerunner 2) Born in Bethlehem 3) Born of a virgin 4) Came out of Egypt 5) Ministry in Galilee 6) Ride into Jerusalem on a donkey 7) Betrayed by a friend 8) Betrayed for 30 pieces of silver 9) Pierced and whipped for man's sin 10) Sneered at and mocked

Some other prophecies fulfilled through Jesus Christ include: (12/1236-1242 & 2/144-166)

1) Jeremiah 23:5 said the Messiah will come from the line of King David. The genealogy of Jesus is

traced back to King David in Luke 3:31 and Matthew 1:6.

2) Daniel 9:25 set the time for the birth of the Messiah, which according to some expert's calculations falls within the general time of when Jesus was born.

3) Psalm 34:20 predicted that none of the Messiah's bones would be broken. John 19:32 reports, "The soldiers ... broke the legs of the first man and the other man who was crucified with him; but coming to Jesus, when they saw he was already dead, they did not break his legs ..." The legs of those crucified were broken to hasten death. They wouldn't be able to use their legs to push themselves up to get air, and thus would suffocate.

4) Psalm 72:10 predicted that kings from the East would offer gifts to the Messiah. According to Matthew 2:1-11 magi (kings) from the east presented baby Jesus with gifts.

5) Isaiah 35:5-6 predicted that the Messiah would heal the blind, deaf, lame and dumb. Throughout the four Gospels there are descriptions of the miracles Jesus performed in healing disease and sickness.

6) Psalm 22:1 record the words, "My God, my God, why hast Thou forsaken me? Far from my deliverance are the words of my groaning." Matthew 27:46 records Jesus' words on the cross to include, "Eli, Eli, Lama Sabachthani?" which means "My God, My God, why hast Thou forsaken me?"

7) Psalm 31:5 predicted the words, "Into Thy hand I commit my Spirit..." Luke 23:46 records

Jesus' last words on the cross as, "Father into Thy hands I commit my spirit."

8) Psalm 69:21 says that the Messiah would be offered gall and vinegar. Matthew 27:34 reports at the time of the crucifixion, "They gave him wine to drink mingled with gall ..." The apostle John referred to it as sour wine (vinegar). Many historians said that this mixture was given to those crucified to help deaden the pain. Jesus refused the offer.

9) Zechariah 11:13 states that the betrayal money would be thrown into the house of the Lord for a potter's field. Matthew 27:5-7 describes how Judas out of remorse returned the silver to the priests by throwing it back into the sanctuary. The Jewish leaders used the silver to buy a potter's field to bury strangers.

10) Psalm 22:16 prophesized that the Messiah's hands and feet would be pierced. Jesus' hands and feet were nailed to a cross.

11) Psalm 22:18 predicted that they would cast lots for the Messiah's garments. Matthew 27:35 relates that the soldiers cast lots for Jesus' tunic while he hung on the cross.

The above are eleven more examples of the sixty major prophecies. Others include; rejected by his people, his side being pierced, buried in a rich man's tomb and darkness over the land. Bible critics have a hard time trying to explain prophecies. When faced with the numerous prophecies about the Messiah that were fulfilled by Jesus they try to present counter arguments. Their explanations are relatively weak and don't hold up when put to the test. The three primary counters to Biblical prophecies are: 1) Jesus purposely set out to fulfill the prophecies 2) Jesus fulfilling the prophecies was a coincidence 3) The New Testament authors manipulated the story to assure the prophecies were fulfilled.

Some claim that Jesus, an Old Testament expert, deliberately set out to fulfill the prophecies in order to convince people he was the promised Messiah. That would make Jesus a liar and fake. He would have agreed to submit to a horrible death for what he knew was false. This isn't credible when considering the character of Jesus. Moreover, many of the prophecies were beyond Christ's ability to control or manipulate. How could he have controlled where and to whom he was born, the events of his betrayal, the manner of his death and the soldiers casting lots for his clothes? In fact of the twenty-one prophecies mentioned in this book there were sixteen for which he could exert no control or influence. This explanation simply doesn't work.

Others claim that it was strictly a coincidence that Jesus fulfilled the prophecies. That might be a possible explanation if he only fulfilled one or two, but not the large number he actually fulfilled. In Chapter 21 of this book mathematician Peter Stone in *Science Speaks* was quoted about the odds of Jesus fulfilling only eight of the prophecies. The chance of one man fulfilling eight is 1 in 10 to the 17th. Stoner uses the analogy of silver dollars spread throughout the state of Texas. The science of probability would rule that out. The odds of one man fulfilling forty-eight of the sixty prophecies are 1 in 10 to the 157th. This is the same as blindly picking a marked atom mixed with atoms equal to a trillion, trillion, trillion, trillion, billion universes the size of our universe. (9/183) It is impossible that Jesus coincidentally fulfilled even eight of the prophecies let alone forty-eight.

Lastly critics say that the New Testament authors manipulated the story so that Jesus would fulfill the prophecies. This flies in the face of all the evidence that proves that the Bible is accurate and trustworthy. That theory would make the Bible a book of intentional lies. All the followers of Jesus would have had to conspire to pull off a major hoax and then willingly die for this hoax. There were too many anti-Jesus Jews and Gentiles living who would have loved to discredit the Gospels as false. They didn't because the Gospel writers depicted the events with integrity. There were non-religious writers who confirmed important portions of the New Testament. Gospel writers knew the truth first hand. They weren't merely following some crazed cult leader like sheep to the slaughter. This wasn't a case of mass suicide like that ordered by Jim Jones in Guyana. They actually saw what was reported and were willing to die for the truth of their message.

Some of the critics that subscribe to the "manipulation by the authors" theory go so far as to accuse them of altering the Old Testament text. They assert Christian scribes copied Old Testament books to make the prophecies correspond to the life of Jesus. They have no evidence of this, but just can't explain the accuracy of Jesus fulfilling the prophecies in any other way. They know that humans can not predict future events with any degree of accuracy, and don't want to accept divine intervention. There is no basis for this indictment of the New Testament authors or early church leaders. Such a giant conspiracy kept secret for 2,000 years for which conspirators were willing to die, doesn't compute. Additionally, there is another major flaw in their theory, the "Dead Sea Scrolls." Many of the scrolls were written before Jesus was born. They confirm that the Old Testament text, including Isaiah, is much the same as we read today.

The evidence is overwhelming that Jesus professed he was God and the promised Savior. The next step to determine is whether his declaration was true or false. Assuming his claim was false, then either he knew or didn't know it was false. There are no other options. It is time to examine those two options in the category of the claim being false. Which one is a reasonable explanation? It is necessary that one of the two provide a rational alternative, otherwise the only other choice is that his claim was true.

Jesus claim to be God was false
and he knew it was false
(Jesus was a liar and evil)

If Jesus wasn't God then two options must be examined. The first is that Jesus Christ knew his claim was false, thus he was an evil man. Even his greatest critics and antagonist would respond, "No way." However, if he claimed to be God and the Savior yet knew that he wasn't, he was a deliberate liar. He would have been a first class con man who deceived men, women and children into following him at significant risk. He would have been the ultimate hypocrite. He repeatedly and aggressively accused others of being hypocrites because of their less than moral motives for their actions. He would have been a fool since he didn't use his celebrity for power or gain. If fact, he was foolish enough to die for the lie. He could have easily avoided a horrible death by simply telling the truth at his trial. He could have recanted the lie and lived. He would have been a phony for healing and forgiving people in God's name. He would have been a demon since he convinced people to trust him with their salvation. He would have been a selfish imposter who lied to everyone including his family and closest friends. In summary; Jesus would have had to been a liar, deceitful, con man, hypocrite, fool, phony, demon, and selfish imposter. In other words Jesus was a very evil man.

Study Jesus' life in detail and see if that description could in any way fit him. The answer has to be "No way." Jesus, in his three years of public ministry was a role model for a man of character. He was good, moral, honest, loving, caring, unselfish, and humble. Everything he did demonstrated these traits. Jesus healed the sick and handicap. He cared for those who were possessed. He spoke out against injustice and hypocrisy. Jesus preached about honesty and love. He loved his enemy and forgave those who hurt him. He spoke the truth even though it meant his death by torture. His ministry was very public and his enemies watched him closely hoping to catch him doing something wrong. The only thing his accusers could charge him with was blasphemy for his claim that he was God and the Messiah. Even Jesus' detractors credit him with being a good moral man of character. One only has to review the Gospels, listen to his followers, and review non-religious material to be convinced that Jesus Christ could not have been an evil man. If you can't accept this option then it must be discarded.

Jesus claim to be God was false, but he didn't know it (Jesus was deluded and seriously mentally ill)

The other option is that Jesus wasn't God but that he thought he was. This means that Jesus was a deluded lunatic. He was insane and belonged in a mental institution. He would have spent three years in public ministry living in a fantasy world. He would have been a schizophrenic escaping from reality. Jesus would have been severely mentally disturbed and no one noticed. Even his most ardent critics and antagonists would have to respond, "No way."

According to mental heath experts and psychiatrists, mentally disturbed persons often exhibit inappropriate emotions, vehement angry outbursts, and are plagued with anxiety. They are often out of touch with reality and paranoid. They, at times, can't carry on a logical conversation, tend to reach faulty conclusions, and are irrational.

Jesus didn't exhibit any of these traits. His emotions like weeping over the death of a friend were normal. His anger expressed against the moneychangers in the Temple was a healthy reaction to evil. His anxiety and stress in the garden knowing of his impending death was natural. He knew throughout his ministry that he was in danger, but never acted paranoid even though he probably had more reason than most. He was always in touch with reality in his words and actions. He understood the Jewish culture and dealt with it effectively. His thinking was rational and speech was clear, powerful and eloquent. He was compassionate, humble, stable, caring, accepting, etc. despite three very demanding years of ministry. He interacted with and was loved by people from all walks of life. Jesus spoke some of the most profound words ever spoken. He actually liberated people from mental bondage. Was he insane, mentally disturbed, paranoid, deluded, and schizophrenic? There can only be one answer. No! Jesus was the model of good sound mental health.

DECISION TIME

Consider thoughtfully what you have just read. The evidence has been presented. Like a juror in a trial, it is now time for deliberation and to make an informed decision. Review the evidence. Was Jesus evil? Was Jesus insane? If your answer to those two questions is no, then the only option left is that Jesus was who he claimed to be; God and the promised Messiah.

The next step is to trust his words and accept him as your Lord and Savior. There will no longer be any question of what happens when you die. You will have received the free gift of eternal salvation. As Jesus said to the thief on the cross who accepted him as his Savior, "Truly I say to you, today you shall be with me in Paradise." Your life will change but you won't be sorry. When I accepted Jesus my main motive was eternal salvation. After maturing somewhat as a Christian I commented to a friend, "I didn't realize all these goodies came with it." What I meant was that my entire life had changed and for the better. You too will probably experience an improved and more contented life here on earth as you mature as a believer. If you are ready and sincere, you can become a follower of Jesus right now. All you have to do is repeat this or a similar prayer using your own words. God will know what's in your heart.

Dear Heavenly Father,

I am a sinner and ask your forgiveness for my sins. I believe that Jesus Christ paid the price for my sins by sacrificing his life on the cross. I accept and am humbled by this free gift as well as your uncon-ditional love. I surrender my life to you and will try to fulfill your purpose for my life. I want Jesus in my heart. I accept Jesus Christ as my Lord and Savior.

If you prayed this prayer then tell someone of your new commitment. I highly recommend you contact a very mature Christian and/or pastor of a Christ-centered, Bible-based church as soon as possible. Get involved in a class, or one on one instruction for a new believer. If you prayed this prayer, then congratulations and welcome into the family. You are welcome to contact me if I can be of any help.

You may not be ready to make a commitment at this time. That's okay. It took me a while. It's better to be certain than insincere. I hope you will make this a priority and contact a pastor in a Christ-centered, Bible-based church as soon as possible. Let the pastor know your situation and ask for some assistance. Please don't put this on the back burner. You are also welcome to contact me.

For those of you who are believers it's time to commit to the Lord's Great Commission, "… to be my witnesses … and even to the remotest part of the earth." Remember at that time North America would have been considered remote. Some evangelist say that it takes something like seven times hearing about Jesus before a non-believer will accept him as their Savior. Make an effort to be one of those seven. Maybe you can plant the seed, water the young sprout or actually be there at the harvest. Either way all the steps are critical. Continue to increase your knowledge and work on your boldness. There is a book I recommend called, "Share Jesus without Fear" by William Fay. It is published by Broadman & Holman Publishers in Nashville, Tennessee. Bill Fay demonstrates a simple and non-threatening method to share Jesus with others.

My address is:
P O Box 3364 Evergreen, Colorado 80437

REVIEW

1. Can you provide examples that clearly show that Jesus said he was God?
2. Name ten Old Testament prophecies about the Messiah that were fulfilled by Jesus.
3. What is the probability of just eight of these prophecies being fulfilled in one man? Give an illustration of this probability.
4. Critics say that Jesus fulfilling Old Testament prophecies was a coincidence. What would be your response?
5. Critics say that Jesus deliberately set out to fulfill the prophecies. What would be your response?
6. Critics say that the Gospel writers manipulated their writing to show that Jesus fulfilled the prophecies. What would be your response?
7. Using logic show how a person can reach the conclusion that Jesus really is God and the Messiah.

PART THREE

COMMON QUESTIONS ABOUT CHRISTIANITY

—m—

CHAPTER 25

INTRODUCTION

—⟋⟍—

In considering religion, a system of beliefs generally dealing with God or gods, it is important to
understand that not all questions can be answered.
Even reasonable answers to some questions will not
necessarily satisfy everyone. No matter how tedious
the study or how deep the research, an individual
will never find adequate answers to all questions.
Accepting this basic premise is important if a person
is to experience peace in his or her spiritual life.

Everyone, whether Christian, Muslim, Jew,
agnostic, or atheist has to take certain things on
faith. Faith can be defined as the acceptance or belief
in something that can't be absolutely proven or
completely explained. Faith is not just reserved for
people involved in organized religion, but is utilized
by everyone, including atheists. They can not prove
there is no God. An atheist accepts that belief based
on some information and a great deal of faith.

There are some who act like faith is a deroga-
tory word or signifies weakness. However, faith is an

everyday reality. I have faith that my wife loves me. All the evidence point to that conclusion, although I can't prove it and I certainly can't explain why. I have faith that the giant 757 will lift off the runway and transport me to another location. I can't prove that will happen nor do I understand the laws of aerodynamics. I have faith the Golden Gate Bridge will remain in tact as I drive across it to San Francisco. I can't guarantee it nor explain how it holds all those cars and trucks while anchored in the bay. I have faith I will wake up in the morning and live another day. I make many of my plans and decisions based on faith. Can you even imagine what this world would be like if people had no faith?

In religious and spiritual growth, people try to obtain as much knowledge as possible and combine that with personal experience, to develop a belief system using faith to fill in the gaps. If people wait for absolute proof and/or the perfect explanation to all questions, they will never develop a belief system. Accept faith as a gift. Don't be ashamed or reluctant to use and acknowledge it.

An illustration of faith can be found in the following dialogue between an atheist professor of philosophy and a Christian student. This was sent to me by e-mail, with the author unknown. I took the liberty of shortening it a bit. During class, the professor asks one of his new students to stand.

"You're a Christian, aren't you son?"
"Yes, I am sir."
"So you believe in God?"

"Absolutely!"

"Tell me," the professor continues, "Do you also believe in Jesus Christ?"

The student responds, "Yes, professor, I do."

The old man stops and looks right at the student, "Science says you have five senses you use to identify and observe the world around you. Have you seen Jesus?"

"No sir, I've never seen Him."

"Then tell us have you ever heard Jesus?"

"No sir, I have not."

"Have you ever felt Jesus, tasted your Jesus or smelled your Jesus? Have you ever had any sensory perception of Jesus Christ or God for that matter?"

"No sir, unfortunately I haven't."

"Yet you still believe in him?"

"Yes."

"According to the rules of empirical, testable, demonstrable protocol, science says your God doesn't exist. What do you say to that?"

"Nothing sir, I have my faith."

The professor shakes his head, "Ah, faith! And that is the problem science has with god. No proof! Only faith and that's a weak basis to rely on, son. You'll have to do better than that."

The student remained quiet for a minute then addresses the professor, "Now tell me professor. Do you teach your students that they evolved from a monkey?"

"If you are referring to the natural evolutionary process, young man, yes of course I do."

"Have you ever observed evolution with your own eyes?"

The professor smiles and shakes his head, no.

"Since no one has ever observed, heard, felt, tasted or smelled the process of evolution at work, are you not teaching your opinion? Thus, you are not acting as a scientist but rather a preacher."

The class went into an uproar.

After the commotion subsided the student turned to the class and facetiously continued, "Now to further the point you were making earlier to the students, let me give you an example of what I mean." The student looked around the room. "Is there anyone in the class who has ever seen the professor's brain?"

The class broke into laughter.

"Is there anyone who has ever heard the professor's brain, felt his brain, touched his brain or smelled the professor's brain?" After waiting a moment the student continued, "No one appears to have done so. According to established rules of empirical, testable, demonstrable protocol, science says that you have no brain. With all due respect if science says you have no brain how can we trust your lectures, sir?"

The room was silent and the professor sheepishly responds, "I guess you'll have to take my lectures on faith."

I will attempt to provide answers to some common questions asked about Christianity. Not all my answers will satisfy everyone. Some questions may have more than one answer, since not all theologians necessarily agree on just one explanation. Remember, we are mere mortals residing in a natural environment, trying to deal with spiritual matters and supernatural concepts. Scientists report that humans use only a small portion of their brain. Some estimate about ten percent. I wonder what would be the potential for understanding, if we could double the capacity to use the brain?

I'm confident that supernatural beings like angels have little or no problems with those issues that cause us such difficulty. An illustration might be a primitive native from the inner jungles of Africa finding himself in New York City. Things that we take for granted would most likely be totally confusing and unexplainable to him. Everything from television to the Empire State Building would be beyond his capacity to understand.

The Bible explains that we will not understand all of God's ways. Isaiah 55:8-9 addresses this with, "for My thoughts are not your thoughts, neither are your ways My ways," declares the Lord, "for as the heavens are higher than the earth, so are My ways higher than your ways, and My thoughts than your thoughts." Paul writes in Romans 11:33, "Oh, the depth of the riches both of the wisdom and knowl-edge of God! How unfathomable are His judgments and unfathomable His ways!"

We must all be careful not to let the lack of understanding or unanswered questions adversely affect our relationship with God. We may not totally understand God's nature or all his ways, but we do have assurance of his love. The bottom line is that Christians are saved by grace through the sacrifice of Jesus Christ. He is the key to salvation and that fact is undeniable in the Bible. Man has often compli-cated what Jesus made very simple, "You shall love the Lord your God with all your heart, and with all your soul, and with all your mind. This is the great and foremost commandment. The second is like it; you shall love your neighbor as yourself. On these two commandments depend the whole Law and the Prophets." (Matthew 22:37-40)

CHAPTER 26

IS THERE A GOD?

O nly a small number of people deny the existence of a deity. Most humans, regardless of
their culture, believe in a supernatural power. Some
cultures believe in more than one god. Usually the
issue isn't whether there is a God, but rather what
is God's nature. Nevertheless, this chapter will deal
with the existence of God to address the views of
atheist.

The following represents an attempt to reproduce
a dialogue between two people discussing the existence of God:

Can you absolutely prove that God exists?
No, I can't absolutely prove that God
exists. Nor can I absolutely prove that Julius
Caesar or George Washington existed, or
even that my husband absolutely loves me.
In fact, there is much we believe that we can't
prove. However, I believe that I can present
credible and persuasive evidence that God

does exist, George Washington existed, and that my husband loves me.

What possible proof or evidence do you have that God exists?

Well for starters, I have the Bible that testifies to the existence of God. Both the Old and New Testaments present compelling evidence and eyewitness accounts that there is a God. Based on the rule of textual criticism, the burden of proof is on you to prove the Bible is false. Thus, the burden of proof is on you to prove there is no God. Therefore, before answering your question, I'd like to ask you if you can provide evidence that God doesn't exist.

Well to start, no one has ever seen, heard, or touched God.

That's not true. According to this world's best seller, the Bible, thousands of people have seen, heard, and touched God through Jesus Christ. You may not know the Bible or totally accept it, but that doesn't disprove God. Have you or any one you know ever seen, heard, or touched Julius Caesar or George Washington? The answer is no, yet you believe the history books about them. I too believe that George Washington and Julius Caesar lived. Nobody seems to have any credible evidence to refute that fact, thus the books should be presumed trustworthy. We have a book that testifies to God's existence which is powerful evidence.

The burden of proof is on you to disprove the Bible. Can you?

That's a whole different issue I'm not prepared to discuss. But if there is a God as you believe, how can he allow evil and suffering to exist? To me that is a contradiction and tends to point to the fact there is no God.

That is a question about God's nature, but not proof he doesn't exist. It is a statement questioning God's motive, purpose, thought process, etc. We can address that issue after we decide if God exists. If he doesn't exist then we don't have to worry about good and evil.

The theory of evolution refutes your Bible's account of creation and God being the creator. Doesn't that disprove God?

Remember, evolution is a theory not a fact. Even if you believe in some degree of evolution, that doesn't disprove God. It's simply a statement about how he might have put his plan into action. After I present evidence that God does exist, I will address evolution in more detail.

How do you account for God's beginning? Where did he come from?

That's a good question. Something had to start it all, which means it could not have been created. The initial cause had to be eternal. We believe that God started it all and thus is eternal. That means he always was and always will be. No matter what you believe we cannot fully understand infinity and eternity as concepts. Whether God or the "Big Bang Theory," we as mere humans with our limited brain capacity cannot comprehend that something always was and always will be. We can't understand dimensions of space and time outside our realm. Something had to exist somehow to establish another something. Something can't come from nothing. The concepts of no beginning, always was, and eternal are bigger than our ability to understand, whether it is about God or scientific theory. This issue assumes everything, including God, is subject to the same limitation of time and space as man. While not totally understandable, the Bible teaches that God exists outside of time and space as we know it. Psalms 90:4, "For a thousand years in Thy sight are like yesterday when it passes by, or as a watch in the night." II Peter 3:8, "But do not let one fact escape your notice, beloved, that with the Lord one day is as a thousand years, and a thousand years as one day." Not being able to understand doesn't disprove God. It simply acknowledges our mental limitations.

I guess to be completely honest; I'll have to agree with science writer, Isaac Asimo, who said, "Emotionally I am an atheist. I don't have the evidence to prove that God doesn't exist but I so strongly suspect he doesn't that I don't want to waste my time." (19/21)

It's too bad you feel that way. Determining for yourself whether there is or is not a God doesn't seem like a waste of time. Believing in God gives meaning to life and faith in an afterlife. What if what the Bible teaches about God is true? Wouldn't you be concerned about where you are, and where you might end up spending eternity?

I've never thought about it. Actually, I don't have to prove something since I'm not asserting anything. You are the one who has the burden proof. So if there isn't any evidence to show God doesn't exist, what is your evidence that he does exist?

Okay, I'll present my case. Let's examine what evidence we have to conclude that God does exist. I believe that God reveals himself in a variety of ways. That includes, but is not limited to the Bible, the law of cause and effect, the logic of order and design, a universal belief, the existence of morals and conscience, and personal experience. Let's consider each of these separately and start with the Bible.

THE BIBLE

To refute the existence of God, an atheist must first prove the Bible is false. Since an atheist has no evidence to deny God, he or she must counter the evidence that God exists. In Chapter 21 we learned that the burden of proof falls on the critic to disprove a document. This is called the rule of literary or textual criticism and is universally used when examining books and other documents. A will is presumed true and accurate, unless someone can produce evidence that it is false and inaccurate. The burden rests on the person contesting the will and not the document itself.

We previously presented compelling evidence that the Bible is accurate and reliable. Based on the evidence and the science of probabilities, it is reasonable to conclude that the men writing the Bible were inspired and guided by a superior intellect we call God. Using the Bible as a resource, it becomes quite apparent that its sixty-six books support the existence of God. In fact, the Bible is all about a personal God and his relationship with mankind. A few examples of the thousands of direct Biblical references to God include:

- "In the beginning God created the heavens and the earth ...." (Genesis 1:1)
- "... The Lord God of your fathers, the God of Abraham, Isaac and ..." (Exodus 3:15)
- "...I am the Lord your God." (Numbers 10:10)
- " The heavens are telling of the glory of God; and their expanse is declaring the work of His hands." (Psalms 19:1)
- " Then you will discern the fear of the Lord, and discover the knowledge of God. For the Lord gives wisdom ...." (Proverbs 2:5-6)
- "But seek first the kingdom of God ...." (Matthew 6:33)

- "… 'You shall love the Lord your God with all your heart …'" (Luke 10:27)
- "… serve a living and true God …" (I Thessalonians 1:9)
- "God so loved the world …" (John 3:16)
- "… He [God] cares for you …." (I Peter 5:7)
- "The one who does not love does not know God, for God is love." (I John 4:8)
- "God is spirit …" (John 4:24)
- "I and the Father are one." (John 10:30)
- "Behold the virgin … they shall call His name Immanuel which translated means, God with us." (Matthew 1:23)
- "… Are you the Son of God, then? And He said to them, "Yes. I am." (Luke 22:70)

Rousseau, considered one of the most important philosophers and writers of the Age of Reason, was impressed with the Scriptures. He knew there was something different about the Bible when he said, "I must confess to you that the majesty of the Scriptures astonishes me; the holiness of the evangelists speaks to my heart and has such striking characters of truth, and is, moreover, so perfectly inimitable, that if it had been the invention of men, the inventors would be greater than the greatest heroes." (6/72)

We have the testimony of the world's greatest book, the Holy Bible and the world's greatest man, Jesus Christ to the existence of God. No philosopher, scientist, or atheist can offer anything even close to disprove the existence of God.

CAUSE AND EFFECT
(1/106-116, 7/9-24, 19/19-26, 27/15-19)

In order for anything to exist it must have either been created by something (cause and effect), self-created, or always existed (eternal). There are no other options.

Law of cause and effect

The law of cause and effect states that there can't be an effect without a cause. If your car has a flat tire (effect), then something like a nail or leaking valve stem (cause) was responsible for the flat. We know that a book must have had an author, and a painting must have had an artist. In our world, everything was caused by something. Something can not come from nothing, thus something must come from another something. This may sound confusing, but is actually a relatively simple law. To exist (effect) an object must have been created by something (cause). This law works well in our physical universe, but something had to have started it all. That leaves self-creation or eternal as options for the very first cause.

Self-creation or spontaneous generation

Many who deny that God exists explain the universe as having self-created or developed from spontaneous generation. Both are basically the same theory and don't pass the test of logic. In order for something to self-create or generate it must first exist. If it didn't pre-exist, then something would have been created from nothing, which is not possible. Self-creation or spontaneous generation is impossible.

This theory defies logic and the law of contradiction which states an object can't both exist and not exist at the same time. Most scientists refute these theories and no longer take them seriously.

A slight modification of this theory is labeled, *creation by chance.* This is popular with evolutionists who don't believe in God. They state that the universe was created by chance. However, chance is not an object, but rather a mathematical concept. Chance relates to the odds of certain things happening. For instance, if you flip a coin you may wonder, "What is the chance that the coin will turn up 'heads?'" Chance has no ability to cause any effect. It has no real existence. To say the universe was created by chance means that it was caused by nothing, which defies logic and not possible. The dictionary defines *chance* as "that which falls out or happens without assignable cause." It further defines chance as a probability or possibility.

Always existed or eternal

The only option left for the initial or first cause is that something always existed or is eternal. That means it had no beginning or end. It is not an effect and thus uncaused. This is a very difficult concept, and totally beyond human capacity to fully understand. This concept is beyond our dimensions of time and space. For something to self-exist or be eternal it must be greater than our universe and be supernatural. It must be independent of our physical universe and the law of cause and effect. Why can't our universe be this eternal uncaused phenomenon? Scientists generally agree and can show that our universe is not eternal. Our universe had a specific beginning and is aging. They believe that the amount of usable energy is decreasing.

In other words, the universe is slowing dying. Our physical universe is subject to the law of cause and effect. That demands that something greater than our universe exists. Consequently, there is a superior supernatural being that is not an effect and thus uncaused. This supernatural being has always existed and was the original cause that created an effect. A person may want to argue the characteristics of this being, but can't logically deny its eternal existence. Most people refer to this being as God. Defining God's nature is a different topic. We may deduce from our universe and its inhabitants, that God is at least supernatural, intelligent, powerful, and moral.

ORDER AND DESIGN

There doesn't seem to be any disagreement that our universe is very complex. The mighty earth, the tiny atom and the human heart all testify to the intricacy of our world. Even though these systems are complicated, they tend to function extremely well. This is because they were designed to serve a specific purpose.

The earth is just the right distance from the sun (approximately 93 million miles). If it was closer, it would be too hot for living things. If it was further, it would be too cold for anything to live. The earth's axis is tilted 23 ½ degrees so that when combined with its motion there is a change of seasons. The earth's water, atmosphere, crust, etc. are all essential in forming and maintaining our planet as we know it. All of these things are arranged in such specific order that it is as if they were intentionally designed that way. (30/earth)

The tiny atom is one of the basic units in matter. The atom is so little that it is more than a million times smaller than the thickness of human hair. The smallest speck must have more than 10 billion atoms to be seen under an ordinary microscope. The atom is made up of even smaller particles called protons, neutrons, and electrons. Atoms form building blocks for chemical elements like hydrogen, oxygen, iron, and lead. For instance, water, often referred to as H_2O is made up of molecules consisting of two atoms of hydrogen and one atom of oxygen. The use of atoms to form the elements is very specific and orderly. (30/atom)

The human heart is a very complex and vital organ necessary to sustain life. If the heart stops functioning so will the human body. The heart is only a little larger than a fist and weighs between nine and twelve ounces. However, this little organ is responsible for maintaining life. If this small organ ceases to function so does the person. The heart contains muscle, valves, veins, arteries, lining, fluid, and chambers all working together for a special purpose. There is no doubt the heart has a very specific design. (30/heart)

In reference the existence of God, this all boils down to a basic question. That is; what caused everything to come about? We have already established that the first cause or creator must be eternal. We now must try to logically conclude whether this eternal thing is most likely; a living intelligent designer who intentionally created the universe with its complex order and design, or mindless inanimate matter that brought about this complex order and design by accident. Educator and author R.C. Sproul in his book, *Reason to Believe* asks, "Even if it were conceivable for inanimate matter to produce life, could it produce intelligence if it were not intelligent itself? Intelligent life is life that has the ability to think and to act in a purposeful way. Can nature do that without intelligence? Can we have purpose by accident? Can we have intention unintentionally? ..." (1/113)

Even Darwin had to admit, "To suppose that the eye with so many parts all working together ... could have formed by natural selection seems, I freely confess, absurd in the highest degree." (7/22) Evolutionist Richard Lewontin from Harvard states that organisms "appear to have been carefully and artfully designed." He calls the perfection of organisms, "the chief evidence of a Supreme Designer." (1/22-23) The probability of life originating from accident according to the book, W*hen Skeptics Ask* is 1 in 10 to the 40,000. (27/22) That is equivalent to impossible. Paul E. Little in his book, *Know Why You Believe,* equates the universe being created by chance to a monkey in a print shop type setting the Gettysburg Address. (7/19) Distinguished astronomer Sir F. Hoyle uses the analogy of creation by chance to a tornado blowing through a junkyard of scattered airline parts and accidentally assembling them into a jet airliner ready for take off. He compares it to the same difficulty as the accidental formation of only one of numerous chains of amino acids in a living cell that contains approximately 200,000. The time required to get all 200,000 amino acids for one human cell to come together by chance would be over 290 times the estimated age of earth. (7/20) In his book, *The Intelligent Universe*, he goes on to state, "As biochemists discover more and more about the awesome complexity of life, it is apparent that its chances of originating by accident are so minute that they can be completely ruled out. Life cannot have arisen by chance." (7/21)

Princeton biology Professor Edwin Carlston states, "The probability of life originating from accident is comparable to the probability of the unabridged dictionary resulting from an explosion in a printing factory." (8/70-71) Albert Einstein said, "My religion consists of a humble admiration of the illimitable superior spirit who reveals himself in the slight details we are able to perceive with our frail and feeble minds. That deeply emotional conviction of the presence of a superior reasoning power, which is revealed in the incomprehensible universe forms my idea of God." (8/70)

Paul E. Little in his book, *Know Why You Believe* writes, "Dr. Robert Jastrow who states that he is an agnostic in religious matters, comments on the theory of the big bang:

Now we see how the astronomical evidence leads to a biblical view of the origin of the world. The details differ, but the essential elements in the astronomical and biblical accounts of Genesis are the same. The chain of events leading to man commenced suddenly and sharply at a definite moment in time, in a flash of light and energy.

Scientists have traditionally rejected the thought of a natural phenomenon which cannot be explained, even with unlimited time and money. There is a kind of religion in science; every event can be explained in a rational way as the product of some previous event; every effect must have its cause. Now science has proven that the universe exploded into existence at a specific moment. It asks, 'What cause produced this effect? Who or what put the matter and energy into the universe?' and science does not answer these questions.

Jastrow concludes with this monumental statement:

> For the scientist who has lived by his faith in the *power of reason*, the story ends like a bad dream. He has scaled the mountains of ignorance; he is about to conquer the highest peak; as he pulls himself over the final rock, he is greeted by a band of theologians who have been sitting there for centuries. (7/24-25)

It would certainly seem more than prob-able that life must have come about by inten-tional design from an intelligent designer, God.

OTHER MEANS GOD IS REVEALED

There are numerous other means by which God is revealed to man. One of these in and of itself may not have the same evidential value as the Bible, the law of cause and effect, or logic of order and design, but together they all contribute to the conclusion that God exists. This book won't go into detail about these other ways God is revealed. You are encour-aged to read the books that have been referenced.

Universal belief (7/18 & 8/78)

Research demonstrates that a belief in God has existed since the beginning of man in all parts of the world and different cultures. Some believe in only one God, while others believe in many gods. All believe in some kind of supernatural being(s). While this is not conclusive proof, it certainly points to the premise that a God or many gods exist. The seven-teenth century noted French physicist Blaise Pascal wrote, "You and I have a God-shaped vacuum at the center of our being." (8/78).

Morals and conscience (7/25-26, 8/74-75, 19/28-29 & 27/22-24)

Humans are born with a conscience or innate ability to detect right and wrong. The conscience can be affected by our culture, but most humans possess a moral code that is quite similar. Dan Story in his book,

Defending Your Faith writes, "Comparative studies in anthropology and sociology reveal a universal standard of behavior in all people regardless of their culture, religion, or their period in history." (19/29) It is universally wrong to murder, steal, cheat, or lie.

If there is no God, where did this built-in system come from? An inanimate object?

If there is no God, then a conscience is not relevant and therefore unnecessary. The fact that we possess a conscience and morals points to the existence of one who enabled us to sense good and evil. In Paul E. Little's book, *Know Why You Believe*, he points out, "C.S. Lewis explains that universally we find people commonly appeal to some sense of right and wrong." He goes on to write, "God's law is not something alien, imposed on us from without, but woven into the very fabric of our being at creation. There is something deep within us that echo God's yes and no, right and wrong. (Romans 2:15 The Message)" (7/25-26) If there is no moral law of good and evil then there can be no value judgments. Thus good and evil cease to exist since they can't be defined.

Meaning of life (1/114-115 & 8/71-72)

If there is no supernatural designer who created humans with a purpose, then life has no true meaning. This would be consistent with the nihilist view that life has no meaning and is an exercise in absurdity. If life is a result of an accident or chance, then we would have to conclude that we exist for no true purpose. We were born from nothing and are destined to nothing, thus how can what's in-between be anything but really nothing? How can this very limited time on earth truly mean something? It is true that most of us want to think our lives count for something. We want to feel we have value and significance. However, if you spend any time in deep thought on this subject, you would probably have to conclude that without a God life is basically meaningless. This desire for significance would then be more based on sentiment than logic and reason.

The novelist Ernest Hemingway wrote, "Life is just a dirty trick, a short journey from nothingness to nothingness." Hemingway decided to cut the journey even shorter by committing suicide. (8/71) This morbid view of life was reflected in Russian novelist Leo Tolstoy's question, "What is life for? To die? To kill myself at once? No, I am afraid. To wait for death till it comes? I fear that even more. Then I must live. But what for? In order to die? And I could not escape from that circle." (8/71) A French existentialist philosopher wrote, "Man is absurd, but he must grimly act as if he were not." (8/71)

Most of us have an animate desire as well as knowledge that our life has true purpose. This innate knowledge can only come from the one who created life and gave it a purpose and meaning. We were created to love God and people. We were created to be good stewards of the earth. We were created to worship God. We were created to live eternally with God. We were created with a definite purpose and true significance as heirs to the King. Our task is to live up to the purpose for which we were created.

Personal experience (7/28, 8/78 & 19/26)

From the days of the Bible to our current times, people have testified to having a personal encounter with God. In some cases these incidences have radically changed lives. These personal experiences have occurred with people from all walks of life and different cultures. It is true these are antidotal stories, but we tend to accept antidotal testimony in other areas of life. We can't prove these people actually had an experience with God, but we also can't disprove it. We can however confirm changed lives. Personal experience constitutes one more indicator that God truly exists. Many people can testify to having a personal experience with God. This can take many forms from a life changing experience, life after death experience, miracles, and/or personal encounters.

CHAPTER 27

CREATION AND EVOLUTION

—⟋⟍⟍⟋—

There are probably very few subjects that have generated more debate and controversy than creation versus evolution. Books have been written by both sides that make compelling arguments using various kinds of data and "facts." Magazines, newspapers, and television regularly cover the topic. They all tend to make it an "either – or" issue. Either God created everything in six literal days or everything was created by chance and there is no God. It has become a God versus no God, and religion versus science debate. That is unfortunate, because this issue can shake some people's faith and keep others from being open to a belief in God. The purpose of this chapter is not to provide you with irrefutable evidence supporting either creation or evolution. I don't think at this time that is possible. You might have noticed that the title of this chapter is *Creation and Evolution* and not, Creation <u>versus</u> Evolution.

The purpose of this chapter is to try to put things into perspective. That is, not to let this one subject blur all the overwhelming evidence supporting Christianity. I feel like people are making this too much of the "either – or" issue. I'm sure this topic will never be resolved to everyone's satisfaction. I am also sure that it really doesn't make any difference. This is not about religion, but rather a science versus science debate. There is no doubt in the heart and minds of most people that God is the creator. The question may be, how did he do it? God knows how he put it all together and someday so will we.

Renowned Scientist and former atheist Francis S. Collins authored the book on evolution called, *The Language of God*. He wrote, "It is time to call a truce in the escalating war between science and spirit, in which the dominate voices have belonged to narrow anti-God materialists and believers who spurn orthodox science." (Wyoming Tribune-Eagle, "Look at God's Evidence", July 22, 2006)

This subject is far too complicated for the average person. This is especially true when you consider some of the greatest scientists and renowned theologians don't agree. There are people who can make sense out of terms like; bacterial flagellum, chloroquine resistance, thermodynamics, entropy, astrophysics, irreducible complexity, anthropic principle, and radioactive decay. I'm not sure I can even pronounce these terms correctly, let alone explain what they mean.

If you're like me, you can read a book favoring macro-evolution and think much of what you read makes sense. The next month you read a book refuting macro, but supporting micro-evolution and much of that makes sense also. Another book refuting evolution as a failed theory could be equally logical. There can be very convincing arguments on all sides of this issue. I guess the basic question to ask is, what difference does it make? One way or the other it doesn't disprove all the evidence supporting the existence of God. Most people clearly understand and believe that we were somehow created by God in his spiritual likeness. The Bible is not a scientific text and should not be treated as one. The Bible doesn't teach the earth is flat or round, the earth is the center of the universe or the earth is 4,000 years old. That's not the purpose of the Bible, but by the same token it does not contradict science.

There are a wide range of views on the topic of creation and evolution. What is the origin of our universe and its inhabitants? Whatever view taken, most feel their theory is supportable and accurate. This chapter will briefly cover some of the more common positions on this controversial topic. If this chapter creates a desire to explore further, I have provided some reference books at the end.

Strict creationist or young earth creationist

The strict creationist believes that the Biblical account of creation is literal. They believe God created the universe and everything in it within six, twenty-four hour days. That is the heavens, sun, moon, stars, earth, water, vegetation, fish, birds, beast, and man all came into existence within a week.

They believe the earth is between 4,000 and 10,000 years old. Although many feel this position flies in the face of scientific evidence, it could be possible. I say possible, because with God anything is possible.

This view of creation can be summed up in the words of President Albert Mohler, of the Southern Baptist Theological Seminary. The August 15, 2005 edition of *Time* magazine quotes Mohler as saying, "Given the human tendency toward inconsistency, there are people who say they hold both positions. But you cannot coherently affirm the Christian truth claim and the dominant model of evolutionary theory at the same time.

"Personally, I am a young Earth creationist. I believe the Bible is adequately clear about how God created the world, and that its most natural reading points to a six-day creation that included not just the animal and plant species but the earth itself. But there have always been Evangelicals who asserted that it might have taken longer. What they should not be asserting is the idea of God's having set the rules for evolution and then stepped back. And even less so, the model held by much of the scientific academy of evolution as the result of a random process of mutations and selection.

"For one thing, there's the issue of human 'descent.' Evangelicals must absolutely affirm the special creation of humans in God's image, with no physical evolution from any nonhuman species. Just as important, the Bible clearly teaches that God is involved in every aspect and moment in the life of His creation and the universe. That rules out the image of a kind of divine watchmaker.

"I think it's interesting that many of the evolution's most ardent academic defenders have moved away from the old claim that evolution is God's means to bring life into being in its various forms. More of them are saying that a truly informed belief in evolution entails a stance that the material world is all there is and that the natural must be explained in purely natural terms. They are saying that anyone who truly feels this way must exclude God from the story. I think their self-analysis is correct. I just couldn't disagree more with their premise."

Critics of strict creationists claim that scientific discoveries, the earth's age, fossils, geographic distribution of species, development of organisms, comparative anatomy, and useless organs all refute the claim of the strict creationist. Critics also question how they account for pre-modern man. Some point out that the story of creation cannot be taken literally because Genesis 1 and 2 have different accounts of the same event.

Some Christians, who believe the Bible is accurate and trustworthy, question taking everything literally. They don't totally accept the saying, "The Bible says it, I believe it, and that settles it." Although reliable, they believe the Bible uses allegories, symbolism, metaphors, and stories to get the message across. They point out that Jesus used parables on a regular basis. There are common expressions that are understood, but not factually accurate. For instance, people talk about the beautiful sunrise or sunset knowing full well that the sun doesn't move, but rather the earth moves causing those beautiful scenes.

There shouldn't be an issue with the strict creationist. It is their right to have that view. It's not up to others to be antagonist toward their belief, and in the big picture it really doesn't matter. Being or not being a strict creationist doesn't necessarily affect spiritually or salvation. However, there are some strict creationists who insist that to be a true Christian, a person must believe as they do. That kind of intolerance tends to bolster the atheist's view that it is either, God and creation — no God and evolution. These strict creationists can hurt the cause of winning souls.

Atheistic evolution

The atheist view of evolution is diametrically opposed to that of the strict creationist. They believe that there was no creator or intelligent designer. This theory is that the universe started billions of years ago with a hot explosive event. Prior to this event, all that existed was smaller than the nucleus of an atom. From this "Big Bang" began the evolutionary process that eventually led to life on earth from a single simple organism. Francis Collins in his book, *The Language of God* writes, "… Richard Dawkins and Daniel Dennett stand out as articulate academics who expend considerable energies to explain and extend Darwinism, proclaiming that an acceptance of evolution in biology requires an acceptance of atheism in theology."

This view of evolution can be summed up in the words of Harvard University psychology professor

Steven Pinker. The August 15, 2005 edition of the *Time* magazine quotes Pinker, "It's natural to think that living things must be the handiwork of a designer. But it was also natural to think that the sun went around the earth. Overcoming naïve impressions to figure out how things really work is one of humanity's highest callings.

"Our own bodies are riddled with quirks that no competent engineer would have planned but that disclose a history of trial-and-error tinkering: a retina installed backward, a seminal duct that hooks over the ureter like a garden hose snagged on a tree, goose bumps that uselessly try to warm us by fluffing up long-gone fur.

"The moral design of nature is as bungled as its engineering design. What twisted sadist would have invented a parasite that blinds millions of people or a gene that covers babies with excruciating blisters? To adapt a Yiddish expression about God: If an intelligent designer lived on Earth, people would break his windows.

"The theory of natural selection explains life as we find it, with all its quirks and tragedies. We can prove mathematically that it is capable of producing adaptive life forms and track it in computer simulations, lab experiments and real ecosystems. It doesn't pretend to solve one mystery (the origin of complex life) by slipping in another (the origin of a complex designer).

"Many people who accept evolution still feel that a belief in God is necessary to give life meaning and to justify morality. But that is exactly backward. In practice, religion has given us stoning, inquisitions and 9/11. Morality comes from a commitment to treat others as we wish to be treated, which follows from the realization that none of us is the sole occupant of the universe. Like physical evolution, it does not require a white-coated technician in the sky."

Critics of this view claim that the atheist totally discounts all the evidence for the existence of God. They put all their eggs in one basket and then close their eyes. It takes much greater faith not believe in God than to believe in God. That is in spite of the impression that some atheists tend to think of themselves as intellectual elitists and Christians as ignorant sheep being lead around by blind faith. Critics also question how non-living material necessary for this "Big Bang" came into being. Referring back to the "Cause and effect" section of Chapter 26, critics use that logic in addressing the "Big Bang" theory. They say it would be necessary that this material be eternal. However, that's not possible because eternal must have no beginning and does not age. Most scientists believe the universe had a beginning and is aging. They believe that the amount of usable energy is decreasing and the universe is slowing dying. Eternal doesn't die but lives forever.

Critics of atheist evolution point out that the beginning of the universe and life is a one-time past event. It can't be re-created, thus science can never prove or disprove how the universe and life developed. They also point out that the chemicals some claim were responsible for evolution didn't exist in the early stages of the universe. The atheist evolution theory assumes that non-living chemicals over a long enough periods of time with the exact right circumstances could produce life. Additionally, critics challenge the theory that all species came from one, since the fossil record does not show that progression. The fossil record shows major groups of animals that are distinct from one another. Critics say that atheistic evolution doesn't take into account the complexity of life and the universe. They point out those endless examples such as the tilt of the earth, the distance from the sun, and the human body as clear signs of an intelligent designer.

Creation and evolution

This view comes with a range of opinions and/or theories. They believe that God is the creator, and that he used varying degrees of evolution to accomplish his creation. These views differ on exactly how heavily God relied on evolution to create the universe and everything in it. They all believe in evolution to some degree. There are those that lean toward "micro-evolution" which accepts small changes within species over time as they adapt to their environment. That accounts for the evolution and variety within species. It also accounts for non essential organs. There is another group that lean toward "macroevolution" which accepts the theory that one species evolved from another. They more fully embrace Darwin's theory of evolution. They believe in God as the creator, but also believe that life developed over time through mutations and natural selection. A closely held view is called "theistic evolution" which fully embraces God and fully embraces evolution. There are other views that are in between micro evolution and macro evolution.

The acceptance of creation and evolution is expressed by Lehigh University Biochemistry Professor Michael Behe. He is quoted in the August 15, 2005 edition of Time magazine, "Sure it's possible to believe in both God and evolution. I'm a Roman Catholic and Catholics have always understood that God could make life any way he wanted to, If he wanted to make it by playing out the natural law, then who are we to object. We were taught in parochial school that Darwin's theory was the best guess at how God could have made life.

"I'm still not against Darwinian evolution on theological grounds. I'm against it on scientific grounds. I think God *could* have made life using apparently random mutation and natural selection. But my reading of the scientific evidence is that he did not do it that way, that there was a more active guiding, I think that we are all descended from some single cell in the distant past but that that cell and later parts of life were intentionally produced as the result of intelligent activity. As a Christian, I say the intelligence is very likely to be God.

"Several Christian positions are theologically consistent with the theory of mutation and selection. Some people believe that God is guiding the process from moment to moment. Others think he set up the universe from a Big Bang to unfold like a computer program. Others take scientific positions that are indistinguishable from those atheist materialists might take but say that their nonscientific intuitions or philosophical considerations or the existence of the mind lead them to deduce that there is a God.

"I used to be part of that last group. I just think now that the science is not nearly as strong as they think."

Alternative

I think that most of us are confused about the entire creation and evolution controversy. It's a very complicated subject with some evidence on all sides. It appears that many are too hung up on this subject when it comes to belief in God. Most feel they must take a position and aggressively try to defend that position. Why? The solution is relatively simple.

I believe there is a God who is also the creator. That belief is based on the evidence outlined in Chapter 26. I'm not sure exactly how God went about creating the universe, earth, and life. Quite frankly, it really doesn't make any difference. How he used or didn't use evolution won't effect my belief in him, my acceptance of Jesus as my Lord, or my salvation. That's what is really important. God knows how he did it, and someday we may understand his ways.

Some books that cover the subject of creation and evolution include: *Defending Your Faith* by Dan Story, *The Case for Faith* by Lee Strobel, *Know Why you Believe* by Paul Little, *When Skeptics Ask* by Norman Geisler and Ron Brooks, *The Language of God* by Francis Collins, *Of Pandas and People* by Percival Davis and Dean Kenyon, and *Darwin's Black Box* by Michael Behe.

CHAPTER 28

HOW CAN A LOVING GOD ALLOW SUFFERING AND EVIL?

—⁓—

We have a tendency to blame God for evil and suffering. We assign all responsibility to him. Why does evil and suffering exist? That is a frequently asked question. There are a variety of responses. This chapter will only address the two that I found most logical. Some try to explain evil by showing how God can use it for good. I agree there are times evil and suffering can bring about positive results, but I don't believe that's why they exist.

Satan is responsible for evil and suffering

When God created beings, he did so for a number of reasons. They included the desire to love and be loved. In order to be loved, he had to permit free will to exist. Otherwise, he would have created robots that would have to be programmed to love. This would be equivalent to an emotionless puppet for which a

267

string could be pulled and a voice responds, "I love you." Is that love? Of course not. God didn't create, nor would we want to be, sterile, mindless, emotionless robots.

In order to love, we must be able to choose not to love. That's free will. That's freedom, which we probably cherish above all other gifts. To give up our freedom would be equivalent to choosing death. Patrick Henry eloquently reflected those feelings with the words, "Give me liberty or give me death." Men and women have repeatedly given their lives fighting for freedom. We should be on our knees every day thanking God for the gift of free will and ability to make choices.

However, along with the gift of freedom comes the responsibility to use it appropriately. Unfortunately, we have all fallen short to varying degrees with poor decisions and sinful behavior. This same free will is what allows us to choose good behavior over bad behavior, to love or to hate, to give life or take life, and to accept God or reject him. Author C.S. Lewis explained, "The sin, both of men and angels, was rendered possible by the fact that God gave them free will: thus surrendering of a portion of His omnipotence ..." (19/172)

God is the creator of all things. He created spirits or supernatural celestial beings we call angels. They were given the gift of freedom of choice. It was a powerful angel that committed the first sin. Satan chose evil over good and rebelled against God. He and his followers were banished from heaven and "thrown down to the earth and his angels were thrown down with him" (Rev.12:9). Jesus said, "I was watching

Satan fall from heaven like lightening." (Luke 10:18) This powerful supernatural being became the ruler over the kingdom of evil. Satan has been called, "adversary", "angel of the abyss", "god of this world", "ruler of demons", "prince of the power of the air", "ruler of the world", "tempter", "the destroyer", "father of lies", "an enemy", "evil one", "world forces of darkness", etc. The earth is his kingdom and demons his followers. Christians are aliens in enemy territory.

It was Satan who tempted Adam and Eve to commit the first human sin. It is Satan who is responsible for evil and suffering, not God. It is Satan, his followers, and man's disobedience that has led to not only man's rebellion but also nature's rebellion. The good creation was blemished and became chaotic. This earth became Satan's evil empire. Cliffe Knechtle writes in *Give Me an Answer,* "God is the giver of life. Satan is the destroyer, the one who tears down life." (8/55) In fact, Satan possesses so much power on earth that he tempted Jesus by offering, "… I will give You this entire domain and its glory [all the kingdoms of the world]; for it has been handed over to me, and I give it to whomever I wish." (Mark 4:5-6) You can't tempt someone if you couldn't produce what you offered. The evil one appears to have dominion over this world. He thrives on evil and suffering.

We have the freedom of choice to follow Satan or God. From God flows love and goodness whereas from Satan flows evil and suffering. Every time we sin we are following Satan's lead. Only God can break

Satan's hold on sin. Someday when we are in God's kingdom we will experience no evil or suffering.

Adam and Eve are responsible for evil and suffering

There are other opinions as to why evil and suffering exist. The most common is that Adam and Eve were responsible for the separation from God because they disobeyed him. That's when evil and suffering entered the Garden of Eden. Man has been sinning ever since. Adam and Eve were created perfect with the freedom to obey or disobey God. They chose to disobey. This was an issue of free will. Evil is a consequence of humanity misusing freedom. In other words, man was responsible for evil and suffering by disobeying God which brought sin into the world. We, through the generations, continue on the marred path initiated by Adam and Eve. Humans can chose good or evil. God created mankind for positive behavior built around love, not negative behavior built around selfishness. Evil and suffering are a result of the freedom God gave humans. Most evil is caused by man as a result of human irresponsibility. If everyone was responsible and practiced unconditional love, evil would be defeated. Someday God has promised he will destroy all suffering and death. He will emerge victorious over Satan. The apostle John in Revelation 21:4 writes, "He will wipe every tear from their eyes. There will be no more death or mourning or crying or pain, for the old order of things has passed away." This will be in God's time, although I'm sure all of us wish it will be sooner than later. In the meantime, we have to accept God's solution and trust him.

CHAPTER 29

IS JESUS THE ONLY WAY TO ETERNAL LIFE WITH GOD?

—◊◊◊—

Some people are offended when Christians claim that the only way to God, the Father is through God, the Son. They complain that Christianity is exclusive. They are right, when it comes to the belief that Jesus is the only way to eternal life with God. Christians need not apologize for that truth. The Bible, Jesus, and his followers were clear and definite on this issue. It's not something that Christians made up so they could have an exclusive club. In fact, missions have been established to invite others into the Christian family. This way of obtaining salvation came directly from God. What happens to non-believers when they die is covered in Chapter 30.

Absolute truth makes some people uncomfortable in this age of relativism. If it doesn't feel right, some people create other explanations that better fit their psyche. This is their truth whether it can be supported or not. They want to believe there are many roads that lead to eternity with God, but have difficulty supporting this view. They claim that it doesn't seem fair for there to only be one way. Maybe in our human capacity or understanding it isn't fair, but on the other side, pure justice without mercy demands that we all be condemned.

Multi-roads (different religions) defies the law of contradiction. All religions are significantly different, teaching different truths considered to be absolute. Christians believe that Jesus is God and the Savior. Muslims do not believe that Jesus is God or the Savior. They both can't be right. The leaders of the different world religions agree that they are all very different in their core beliefs. Each one would attest that they are the one true religion. However they all can't be right. That would go against the law of logic and principle of either/or. The question is, which one right? It can only be one. The Bible which has already been established as reliable and trustworthy makes it clear which one. It also makes it clear that Jesus Christ is as he said, "I am the way, and the truth and the life. No one comes to the father, but through Me." (John 14:6)

The Bible teaches that God's kingdom is a place of pure perfection with not a single blemish. The one (Satan) who attempted to stain heaven was banished along with his followers. In order for heaven to remain in the state of pure perfection, mankind is barred from entry. That is because we are all sinners and thus imperfect. In our current state we would place a blemish in heaven. That would make it no different than earth

274

(Satan's world), and a place God could not reside. Victory would belong to Satan. Somehow we must be made perfect or sinless in order to enter God's kingdom. God because of his love sent his son, the unblemished perfect lamb to pay the ransom for our sins. Christ took on our transgressions and paid the price with a horrible death. He suffered and died for us, so that we could enter heaven as unblemished children of God. In order to accept this gift of grace and escape God's justice, we must confess our sins as well as accept the sacrifice of Jesus as our Lord and Savior.

Jesus assumed our guilt so that we could be set free and have eternal life with God. There is a story about a judge that illustrates this point. In a remote small town there was only one judge who handled all criminal and civil matters in that juris-diction. This judge was known for his wisdom, integrity and sense of justice. He was also known as a loving and merciful man. The judge handed out justice according to the law in keeping with what the wrong-doer deserved. After nine years on the bench, tragedy struck his family. His nineteen year old son committed first degree murder and pled guilty to the offense. The remorseful son asked for forgive-ness, but knew he faced the death penalty. On the day of sentencing he was brought before his father, the judge. He stood before the bench and waited for his father to hand down the sentence. His father with tears in his eyes looked down at his only son. With his voice quivering, the judge pronounced, "I hereby sentence you to death by hanging." The son nodded and turned to be taken out of the court room. At the same time the judge stood up from the bench and removed his robe. He then went down to the bailiff and with arms outstretched said, "Although justice demands death, my love and mercy compels me to die in his place. Take me to the gallows and set my son free." Justice and love make for a very tough partnership. Just ask God who gave his only son for all of us undeserving sinners.

Cliffe Knechtle in his book, *Give Me an Answer* provides another illustration, "During World War 2 the guards at a Japanese prisoner-of-war camp would take the English soldiers out into the fields to do hard manual labor. At the end of the day the guards lined up the English prisoners and counted the tools. They found that one shovel was missing. A guard called out, 'Who stole the shovel?' No one responded. The Japanese guard cocked his rifle and said, 'All die! All die!'

"Suddenly one Scottish soldier stepped forward and said,. 'I stole the shovel.' Instantly he was shot dead. His comrades gathered up his body and the remaining tools and went back to the prisoner-of-war compound. Back in the prison camp, the Japanese guards counted the tools again. They found that no shovel was missing. The Scottish soldier had sacrificed his life so his buddies might live."

The answer to the question in the title of this chapter is, "yes." The New Testament is clear on the issue of salvation and eternity. It does not leave any room for doubt or interpretation. Jesus Christ is "The Way" and the only way. There are numerous Biblical passages that confirm this truth. Jesus himself, the

Son of God, made it abundantly clear that he is the road to salvation and eternal life with God. A few examples include:

Words of Jesus

Jesus states, "Truly, truly, I say to you, he who hears My word, and believes Him who sent Me, has eternal life, and does not come into judgment, but has passed out of death into life." (John 5:24)

Jesus said, "I am the way, and the truth and the life; no one comes to the Father, but through me." (John 14:6)

Jesus stated, "Everyone therefore who shall confess me before men, I will also confess him before My Father who is in heaven. But whoever shall deny Me before men, I will also deny him before My Father who is in heaven." (Matthew 10:31-32)

Jesus explained to Martha, "... I am the resurrection and the life; he who believes in Me will live even if he dies ..." (John 11:25)

Jesus relayed that, "For God so loved the world that He gave His only begotten Son, that whoever believes in Him should not perish, but have eternal life." (John 3:16)

Jesus told Nicodemus, "Truly, truly, I say to you, unless one is born of water and the spirit, he cannot enter into the kingdom of God. That which is born of the flesh is the flesh and that which is born of the Spirit is spirit." (John 3:5-6)

The followers of Christ, many of whom died for their faith, testified that Jesus was "The Way." Some examples include:

Words of his followers

The great historian Luke wrote, "And there is salvation in no one else; for there is no other name under heaven that has been given among men, by which we must be saved." (Acts 4:12)

Paul wrote to the Church at Rome, "for, 'Everyone who calls on the name of the Lord will be saved.'" (Romans 10:13)

Luke also relayed the story of the jailer who asked what he must do to be saved. Paul and Silas answered the jailer and his family, "Believe in the Lord Jesus, and you shall be saved, you and your household." (Acts 16:30-31)

Paul, the former persecutor of Christians turned apostle told the church at Rome, "That if you confess with your mouth that Jesus is Lord, and believe in your heart that God raised Him from the dead, you shall be saved." (Romans 10:9) (NI)

One of original apostles, John wrote, "These things I have written to you who believe in the name of the Son of God in order that you may know that you have eternal life." (I John 5:13)

Peter, the leader of the apostles wrote, "Blessed be the God and father of our Lord Jesus Christ, who according to His great mercy has caused us to be born again to a living hope through the resurrection of Jesus Christ from the dead, to obtain an inheritance which is imperishable and undefiled and will not fade away, reserved in heaven for you." (I Peter 3-4)

John wrote to his friends and closed the letter with, "I write these things to you who believe in the name of the Son of God so that you will know that you have eternal life." (1 John 5:13) (NI)

We may not understand or like the answer, but nevertheless it is the truth. You can question God's motives, plan, tactics, purpose, etc., but that doesn't change the fact that the only way to God is through Jesus. You may be thinking that if you were god, you would develop a number of roads to heaven. But the fact is, you are not God, nor do we always understand his ways. Don't try to totally understand it, but rather accept it. You can ask God why once you are safely in his kingdom.

If there were other ways to eternal life with God, then Jesus would have suffered and died in vain. That would mean that His sacrifice wasn't necessary, and that the passion of the Christ was all for nothing.

CHAPTER 30

WHAT HAPPENS TO NON-CHRISTIANS WHEN THEY DIE?

—⟋⟍⟍—

One of the frequently asked questions is what happens to non-Christians when they die? The truth of the matter is that even within the Christian community there is a variety of opinions. The most honest answer is that we are not exactly sure what happens or how it happens. We have to trust that the God of love, mercy, and justice will do what is right. We do know that God offers a free eternal life insurance policy through His Son. If you know Jesus, but have turned down God's offer you should reconsider. Accepting this gift of assured salvation is like taking an express train to paradise. You know you make it. You or your family won't have to wonder. What exactly happens to non-believers is a question to be considered using the Bible as the guide. Unfortunately it does not appear that the Bible is definitive on the issue. I will provide a number of options, all of which have at least some Biblical backing. You may believe in more than just one. For instance, you may believe that everyone will have one last opportunity to accept Jesus, except evil people who will be eternally punished. My personal answer is, "I don't know what happens to non-believers, but I do know what happens to believers. Why take the chance?"

Some may ask a Christian, "What if you are wrong?" The response might be, "So what? The worst case is that I've probably lead a more contented life following Jesus, then if I hadn't followed him."

The Christian then may ask a non-believer, "But what if you are wrong?"

OPTION ONE

Everyone will be given an opportunity to accept Jesus before the final judgment. This view could be considered supported by at least the following Scriptures:

- Jesus told some Jews who were challenging him, "I tell you the truth; a time is coming and has now come when the dead will hear the voice of the Son of Man and those who hear will live." (John 5:25 NI)
- Jesus continues, "Do not be amazed at this, for the time is coming when all who are in their graves will hear his voice and come out – those who have done good will rise to live, and those who have done evil will rise to be condemned." (John 5:28-29 NI)

- Paul wrote, "... that at the name of Jesus every knee shall bow, in heaven and on earth and under the earth, and every tongue confess the Jesus Christ is Lord to the glory of God the Father." (Philippians 2:10-11 NI)

- Peter wrote, "The Lord is not slow in keeping his promise, as some understand slowness. He is patient with you, not wanting anyone to perish, but everyone to come to repentance." (2 Peter 3:9)

- Paul wrote to Timothy, "Even though I was once a blasphemer and a persecutor and a violent man, I was shown mercy because I acted in ignorance and unbelief." (I Timothy 1:13 NI)

- In another letter to Timothy, Paul wrote, "This is good and pleases God the Savior, who wants all men to be saved and to come to the knowledge of truth." (1 Timothy 2:3-4 NI)

- Matthew reported that at the exact time Jesus died, "The tombs broke open and the bodies of the many holy people who had died were raised to life." (Matthew 27:52 **NI**)

- Jesus responding to Jews who were questioning him said, "Your father Abraham rejoiced at the thought of seeing my day; he saw it and was glad." (John 8:56)

OPTION TWO

When life ends there will come a time during which all men will be judged. That judgment will determine a person's fate. Some of the Scriptures that support a final judgment are:

- Jesus states, "Nevertheless I say to you, it will be more bearable for Tyre and Sidon on the Day of Judgment than for you." (Matthew 11:22)

- Jesus told the Pharisees, "For by your words you will be acquitted, and by your words you will be condemned." (Matthew 12:37 NI)

- While teaching the people in the temple, Jesus said, "… such men will be punished more severely." (Mark 12:40 NI)

- Jesus talking to the crowds said, "But he who denies me before men will be denied before the angels of God." (Luke 12:9)

- In the same message, Jesus discussed degrees of punishment with this example, "That the servant who knows his master's will and does not get ready or does not do what the master wants will be beaten by many blows. But the one who does not know and does things deserving punishment will be beaten with few blows." (Luke 12:47-48 NI)

- Jesus told Nicodemus, "He who believes in Him is not judged; he who does not believe has been judged already,…" (John 3:18)

- Jesus told the Jews who were challenging him, "For not even the Father judges anyone, but He has given all judgment to the Son." (John 5:22)

- Jesus spoke these words to the crowd at the Passover gathering, "But all who reject me and my message will be judged at the Day of Judgment by the truth I have spoken." (John 12:48 NL)

- When Paul was preaching in Athens he stated, "For he [God] has set a day when he will judge the world with justice by the man [Jesus] he has appointed, ..." (Acts 17:31 NI)

- Paul wrote to the Church at Rome, "... for there is going to come a day of judgment when God, the just judge of all the world, will judge all people according to what they have done." (Romans 2:5-6 NL)

- Paul wrote to the Church at Corinth, "For we will all appear before the judgment seat of Christ, that each one may receive what is due him for the things done while in the body, whether good or bad." (2 Corinthians 5:10 NI)

- John, in the book of Revelation, told of this vision of the final judgment, "Then I saw a great white throne and him who was seated on it ... And I saw the dead, great and small, standing before the throne, and the books were opened. Another book was opened, which is the book of life. The dead were judged according to what they had done as recorded in the books. The sea gave up the dead that were in it, and death and Hades gave up the dead that were in them, and each person was judged according to what he had done. Then death and Hades were thrown into the lake of fire. The lake of fire is the second death. If anyone's name was not found written in the book of life, he was thrown into the lake of fire." (Revelation 20: 11-14 **NL**)

OPTION THREE

Non-believers will be denied the ultimate experience of being in the presence and glory of God. Scriptures that tend to support this view are the following:

- Jesus at a dinner party taught the guest by using a parable about a banquet, "For I tell you, not one of those men who were invited will get a taste at my dinner." (Luke 14:24)
- Jesus talking with Nicodemus told him, "I tell you the truth, no one can see the kingdom of God unless he is born again." (John 3:3 NI)
- After healing the Roman officer's young servant, Jesus was impressed with the soldier's faith. He explained that believing Gentiles would be saved, whereas non-believing Jews would not, "And I tell you this, that many Gentiles will come from all over the world and sit down with Abraham, Isaac and Jacob at the feast in the Kingdom of Heaven. But many Israelites—those for whom the kingdom was prepared—will be cast into the outer darkness where there will

be weeping and gnashing of teeth." (Matthew 8:11-12 NL)

- Jesus was explaining to the crowd to be ready using a parable of a servant. He explains that if the master comes when not expected and finds an evil servant then, "… will cut him in pieces and assign him a place with the unbelievers." (Luke 12:46)
- Jesus was preaching and responded to a question about being saved, "Strive to enter by the narrow door; for many, I tell you, will seek to enter and will not be able." (Luke 13:24)
- Paul wrote to the Thessalonica Church, "They will be punished with everlasting destruction and shut out from the presence of the Lord and from the majesty of his power." (2 Thessalonians 1:9 Ni)

OPTION FOUR

Non-believers who die physically will likewise die spiritually. Their soul will simply cease to exist. This view could be considered supported by the following Scriptures:

- Jesus teaching his disciples stated, "And how do you benefit if you gain the whole world but lose your own soul in the process?" (Matthew16:26 NL)
- Jesus was giving his twelve disciples instructions when he said, "Do not be afraid of those who kill the body but cannot kill the soul. Rather, be afraid of the One who can destroy

both the soul and body in hell." (Matthew 10:28 NI)

- Jesus talking with some Jews who were challenging him said, "I tell you the truth, whoever hears my word and believes him who sent me has eternal life and will not be condemned; he has crossed over from death to life." (John 5:24 NI)

- Jesus responded to the Pharisees, "I told you that you would die in your sins; if you do not believe that I am the one I claim to be, you will indeed die in your sins." (John 8:24 NI)

- In comforting Martha, the sister of Lazarus, Jesus said, "I am the resurrection and the life; he who believes in Me will live even if he dies, and everyone who lives and believes in Me will never die ..." (John 11:25)

- Paul wrote to the Corinthians, "If there is no resurrection of the dead, then Christ has not been raised. And if Christ has not been raised, then your faith is useless, and you are still under condemnation for your sins. In that case, all who have died believing in Christ have perished." (1 Corinthians 15:16-18)

- Paul wrote to the Thessalonians, "... I want you to know what will happen to the Christians who have died so you will not be full of sorrow like people who have no hope.... God will bring back with Jesus all the Christians who have died." (1 Thessalonians 4:13-14 NL)

- Peter wrote, "… They [wicked] are like brute beast, creatures of instinct, born only to be caught and destroyed, and like the beasts they too will perish." (2 Peter 2:12 NI)
- Paul wrote to the Church at Rome, "For the wages of sin is death, but the gift of God is eternal life in Jesus Christ our Lord." (Romans 6:23)
- Jesus said to his hecklers, "I tell you the truth, if anyone keeps my word, he will never see death." (John 8:51 NI)

OPTION FIVE

Those who are evil shall be sent to eternal damnation referred to as hell. Scriptures that support this position are:

- Jesus preaching the *Sermon on the Mount* said, "… and if you curse someone, you are in danger of the fires of hell." (Matthew 5:22 NL)
- Jesus continued in the sermon by saying, "And if your right hand causes you to sin, cut it off and throw it away. It is better for you to lose one part of your body than for the whole body to go into hell." (Matthew 5:30 NI)
- Jesus using a parable to make his point said, "This is how it will be at the end of the age. The angels will come and separate the wicked from the righteous, and throw them into the fiery furnace, where there will be weeping

and gnashing of teeth." (Matthew 13:49-50 NI)

- Matthew, an eyewitness, reports that Jesus made the following statements, "... how will you [snakes and vipers] escape being condemned to hell?" "... depart from me, you who are cursed, into the eternal fire prepared for the devil and his angels." "Then they [the evil] will go away to eternal punishment but the righteous to eternal life." (Matthew 23:33, 25:41, and 25:46 NI)

- Paul wrote to the Church at Rome, "But to those who are self-seeking and reject the truth and follow evil, there will be wrath and anger. There will be trouble and distress for every human who does evil ..." (Romans 2:8-9 NI)

- Jude wrote, "... and are a warning of eternal fire that will punish all who are evil." (Jude 1:7 NL)

- Peter wrote, "For if God did not spare the angels when they sinned, but sent them to hell, putting them in gloomy dungeons to be held for judgment; and if he didn't spare ..." (2 Peter 2:4-5 NI)

OPTION SIX

Not sure what exactly will happen to non-believers. However, trust that God who is loving, merciful and just will do the right thing.

- The Bible is filled with verses describing God's sense of justice, fairness, and righteousness. It is also filled with verses describing God's loving nature and many acts of mercy involving mankind. I don't think these characteristics of God are in question. How that translates to non-believers, only God knows. What is loving and merciful justice in his eyes?

- Renowned Christian writer C.S. Lewis remarks, "The truth is God hasn't told us what His arrangements about other people are. We do know that no man can be saved except through Christ ..."

- Moses in Genesis 18:25 writes about Abraham's conversation with God, "Far be it from you to do such a thing – to kill the righteous with the wicked, treating the righteous and wicked alike. Far be it from you! Will not the judge of all earth do right?"

- King David in Psalms 145:17 wrote, The Lord is righteous in all His ways and loving toward all He has made .... The Lord watches over all who love Him, but all the wicked He will destroy."

- This is something everyone is going to have to deal with individually. Personally I chose to follow the lead of Joshua who said, "But if serving the Lord seems undesirable to you, then choose for yourselves this day whom you will serve, ... But as for me and my household, we will serve the Lord." (Joshua 24:15 NI)

I hope this book has been helpful and enlightening.

May God bless you in your quest for knowledge and the truth!

REFERENCE MATERIAL

—ᴟ—

1) R. C. Sproul, *Reason to Believe* (Grand Rapids, MI: Zondervan Publishing House, 1979).

2) Josh McDowell, *Evidence that Demands a Verdict* (San Bernardino, CA: Here's Life Publishers, 1979)

3) Josh McDowell, *More Evidence that Demands a Verdict* (San Bernardino, CA: Here's Life Publishers, 1981)

4) Josh McDowell, *A Ready Defense* (Nashville, TN: Thomas Nelson, Inc.,1993)

5) Josh McDowell, *More than a Carpenter* (Wheaton, IL: Tyndale house Publishers, 1977)

6) Josh McDowell and Don Stewart, *Answers to Tough Questions* (San Bernardino, CA: Here's Life Publishers, 1980)

7) Paul E. Little, *Know Why you Believe* (Colorado Springs, CO: Scripture Press Publications, 1980)

8) Cliffe Knechtle, *Give me an Answer* (Downers Grove, IL: Inter-Varsity Press, 1986)

9) Lee Strobel, *The Case for Christ* (Grand Rapids, MI: Zondervan Publishing House, 1998)

10) Lee Strobel, *The Case for Faith* (Grand Rapids, MI: Zondervan Publishing House, 2000)

11) Merrill Unger, *Unger's Bible Dictionary* (Chicago, IL: Moody Press, 1981)

12) *New American Standard Bible, The Open Bible Edition* (Nashville, TN: Thomas Nelson Publishers, 1979)

13) C. S. Lewis, *Mere Christianity* (Westwood, Barbour and Company, 1952)

14) *The Zondervan Pictorial Encyclopedia of the Bible* (Grand Rapids, MI: Zondervan Publishing House, 1982)

15) Jeff Rovin, *Fascinating Facts from the Bible* (Boca Raton, FL: American Media Mini Mags, 2001)

16) Peter Kreeft and Ronald K. Tacelli, *Handbook of Christian Apologetics* (Downers Grove, IL: InterVarsity Press, 1994)

17) William Fay with Linda Evans Shepherd, *Share Jesus Without Fear* (Nashville, TN: Broadman and Holman Publishers, 1999)

18) Ralph Herring and Frank Stagg, *How to Understand the Bible* (Nashville, TN: Broadman Press, 1974)

19) Dan Story, *Defending Your Faith* (Grand Rapids, MI: Kregel Publications, 1997)

20) F.F. Bruce, *Archaeological Confirmation of the New Testament* (Grand Rapids, MI: Baker Book House, 1969)

21) F.F. Bruce, *The New Testament Documents: Are They Reliable* (Downers Grove, IL: InterVarsity Press, 1964)

22) W. F.Arndt, *Does the Bible Contradict Itself* (Chicago, IL: The University of Chicago Press, 1950)

23) Ian Wilson, *Jesus: The Evidence* (San Francisco, CA: Harper's Publishing 1988)

24) Frederic Kenyon, *The Bible and Archaeology* (New York, NY: Harper's Publishing, 1940)

25) William F Albright, *Recent Discoveries in Bible Lands* (New York, NY: Funk and Wagnalls, 1955)

26) Gospelcom.net, Faith Facts

27) Norman Geisler and Ron Brooks, *When Skeptics Ask* (Grand Rapids, MI: Baker Books, 1996)

28) Archer L. Gleason, *The Encyclopedia of Bible Difficulties* (Grand Rapids, MI: Zondervan Publishing house, 1982)

29) Robert A. Baker, *Summary of Christian History* (Nashville, TN: Broadman Press, 1959)

30) *World Book Encyclopedia* (Chicago, IL: World Book Inc., 2003)

Printed in the United States
200029BV00001B/4-99/A

9 781600 349881